Quick & Easy
Low Fat

p

Contents

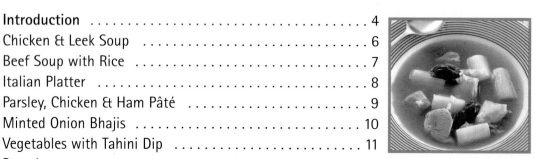

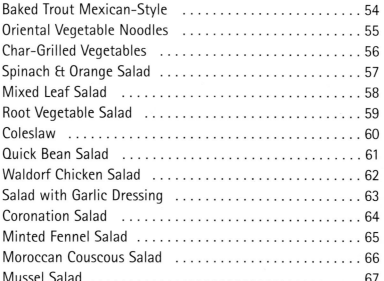

Introduction

Healthy eating means that you can enjoy all of your favourite foods and still keep in great shape. These carefully selected recipes will show you how you can eat nutritious, filling, well-balanced meals, full of flavour and low in fat. Packed full of dishes that are quick and simple to prepare, *Low Fat* provides an array of healthy, low-fat dishes for you, your family and your guests to enjoy.

Reducing Your Fat Intake

Reducing the fat content in our diet is very easy, and the benefits are myriad. Not only do supermarkets provide a variety of healthy alternatives to full-fat ingredients, such as reduced-fat dairy products, but the variety of fresh fruit and vegetables available provides excellent sources of essential vitamins. The easiest and quickest way to reduce your fat calorie intake is to change from full-fat milk, cream, cheese and yoghurt to a low- or reduced-fat equivalent. Semi-skimmed milk, for example, has all the nutritional benefits of whole milk but 10 g/^{1}/$_3$ oz of fat per pint compared with 23 g/^{3}/$_4$ oz of fat per pint in whole milk.

The Benefits of Fat

Reducing the level of fat in your diet is synonymous with losing weight. Yet there are many benefits in eating the right types of fat of which many dieters are unaware. It is important to remember that we all need to include a certain amount of fat in our daily intake to function properly. Essential fatty acids are required in order to build cell membranes and for other vital bodily functions. Our brain tissues, nerve sheaths and bone marrow need fat, and we also need fat to protect our organs such as our liver, kidneys and heart.

When is Fat Bad?

Fat is bad when we consume a high level of it in our diet. Too much fat increases the risk of developing coronary disease, diabetes and even cancer — and, of course, it can lead to obesity. But high-fat diet-related illnesses are not limited to those who are overweight.

Nutritionists suggest that we should aim to cut our intake of fat to 27–30 per cent of our total daily calorie intake. If your average diet totals 2000 calories, this will mean eating no more than about 75 g/2^3/$_4$ oz of fat a day. As a guide, most people consume 40 per cent of their daily calories in the form of fat. However, you should always consult your family doctor if you are being treated for any medical condition before you begin a new regime.

Different Types of Fat

Fats are made up of a combination of fatty acids and glycerol. Fatty acids consist of a chain of carbon atoms linked to hydrogen atoms. The way these are linked determines whether they are saturated or unsaturated fats, and consequently if they should be avoided or not.

Saturated fats. These are easily recognisable. Saturated fats are solid at room temperature and are mainly found in animal products, such as meat and dairy foods, although some vegetable oils, including palm and coconut oil, contain them.

Our body has difficulty processing these saturated fats and, as a result, it tends to store them. They increase cholesterol levels in the bloodstream, which can in turn increase the risk of heart disease. It is therefore important to reduce the level of saturated fats in the diet: they should comprise no more than 30 per cent of the total fat intake or no more than nine per cent of the total energy intake.

Unsaturated fats. These are normally liquid or soft at room temperature and are thought to reduce the level of cholesterol in the bloodstream. There are two types of unsaturated fats: monounsaturated and polyunsaturated. The former are mainly found in vegetables, but they also occur in oily fish, such as mackerel. The latter are only found in oily fish and seed oils.

Cooking Methods

The way we cook our food is one of the most important factors in ensuring a healthy, low-fat diet. In general, steaming is the best way to cook vegetables to preserve their goodness. Boiling can, for example, destroy up to three-quarters of the vitamin C present in green vegetables. This guide will help you to choose the healthiest way to cook your dish, while maintaining optimum flavour and colour.

KEY

 Simplicity level 1 – 3 (1 easiest, 3 slightly harder)

 Preparation time

 Cooking time

- **Frying**. This is the most fat-rich method of cooking. Yet, surprisingly, deep-frying the food absorbs less fat than shallow-frying. To cut down on fat intake, buy a good quality, non-stick frying pan as you will need less fat, and use a vegetable oil, high in polyunsaturates. A good method is to stir-fry food: you require little oil as the food is cooked quickly over a high heat.

- **Grilling**. This is a good alternative to frying, producing a crisp, golden coating whilst keeping food tender and moist. Ingredients with a delicate texture and which can easily dry out, such as white fish or chicken breasts, will require brushing with oil. Marinating can reduce the need for oil. Always cook on a rack, so that the fat drains away.

- **Poaching**. This is ideal for foods with a delicate texture or subtle flavour, such as chicken and fish, and it is fat free. The cooking liquid can make the basis of a nutritious and flavoursome sauce: try alternative liquids such as stock, wine and acidulated water, flavoured with herbs and vegetables.

- **Steaming**. This is also fat-free and is becoming a popular method of cooking meat, fish, chicken and vegetables. Ingredients maintain their colour, flavour and texture, fewer nutrients are leached out. An additional advantage is that when meat is steamed, the fat melts and drips into the cooking liquid – this should not then be used for gravy.

- **Braising and stewing**. Slow-cooking techniques produce succulent dishes that are especially welcome in winter. Trim all visible fat from the meat and always remove the skin from the chicken.

- **Roasting**. Fat is an integral part of this cooking technique and without it meat or fish would dry out. Try standing meat on a rack over a roasting tray so that the fat drains off. Do not use the meat juices for gravy.

- **Baking**. Many dishes are fat free. Foil-wrapped parcels of meat or fish are always delicious. Add fruit juice or wine instead of oil or butter for a moist texture.

- **Microwave**. Food cooked in this way rarely requires additional fat.

Chicken & Leek Soup

This satisfying soup can be served as a main course. You can add rice and (bell) peppers to make it even more hearty, as well as colourful.

NUTRITIONAL INFORMATION

Calories 183	Sugar 4g
Protein 21g	Fats 9g
Carbohydrates 4g	Saturates 5g

 5 MINS   1¼ HOURS

SERVES 4–6

INGREDIENTS

25 g/1 oz/2 tbsp butter

350 g/12 oz boneless chicken

350 g/12 oz leeks, cut into 2.5-cm/
    1-inch pieces

1.2 litres/2 pints/5 chicken stock

1 bouquet garni sachet

8 pitted prunes, halved

salt and white pepper

cooked rice and diced (bell) peppers
    (optional)

1 Melt the butter in a large saucepan.

2 Add the chicken and leeks to the saucepan and fry for 8 minutes.

3 Add the chicken stock and bouquet garni sachet and stir well.

4 Season well with salt and pepper to taste.

5 Bring the soup to the boil and simmer for 45 minutes.

6 Add the prunes to the saucepan with some cooked rice and diced (bell) peppers (if using) and simmer for about 20 minutes.

7 Remove the bouquet garni sachet from the soup and discard. Serve the chicken and leek soup immediately.

VARIATION

Instead of the bouquet garni sachet, you can use a bunch of fresh mixed herbs, tied together with string. Choose herbs such as parsley, thyme and rosemary.

Beef Soup with Rice

Strips of tender lean beef are combined with crisp water chestnuts and cooked rice in a tasty beef broth with a tang of orange.

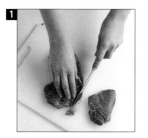

NUTRITIONAL INFORMATION

Calories 210	Sugar 4g
Protein 20g	Fats 5g
Carbohydrates . . .21g	Saturates 2g

🕙 25 MINS   🕙 25 MINS

SERVES 4

I N G R E D I E N T S

350 g/12 oz lean beef (such as rump or sirloin)

1 litre/1¾ pints/1 quart beef stock

1 cinnamon stick, broken

2 star anise

2 tbsp dark soy sauce

2 tbsp dry sherry

3 tbsp tomato purée (paste)

115 g/4 oz can water chestnuts, drained and sliced

175 g/6 oz/3 cups cooked white rice

1 tsp zested orange rind

6 tbsp orange juice

salt and pepper

TO GARNISH

strips of orange rind

2 tbsp chives, snipped

1 Carefully trim away any fat from the beef. Cut the beef into thin strips and then place into a large saucepan.

2 Pour over the stock and add the cinnamon, star anise, soy sauce, sherry, tomato purée (paste) and water chestnuts. Bring to the boil, skimming away any surface scum with a flat ladle. Cover the pan and simmer gently for about 20 minutes.

3 Skim the soup with a flat ladle to remove any more scum. Remove and discard the cinnamon and star anise and blot the surface with absorbent kitchen paper to remove any fat.

4 Stir in the rice, orange rind and juice. Check the seasoning. Heat through for 2–3 minutes before ladling into warm bowls. Serve garnished with strips of orange rind and snipped chives.

COOK'S TIP

Omit the rice for a lighter soup that is an ideal starter for an Oriental meal of many courses. For a more substantial soup that would be a meal in its own right, add diced vegetables such as carrot, (bell) pepper, sweetcorn or courgette (zucchini).

Italian Platter

This popular hors d'oeuvre usually consists of vegetables soaked in olive oil and rich, creamy cheeses. Try this great low-fat version.

NUTRITIONAL INFORMATION

Calories 198   Sugars 12g
Protein ....12g   Fat 6g
Carbohydrate ...25g   Saturates 3g

    10 MINS   0 MINS

SERVES 4

INGREDIENTS

125 g/4½ oz reduced-fat Mozzarella cheese, drained

60 g/2 oz lean Parma ham (prosciutto)

400 g/14 oz can artichoke hearts, drained

4 ripe figs

1 small mango

few plain Grissini (bread sticks), to serve

DRESSING

1 small orange

1 tbsp passata (sieved tomatoes)

1 tsp wholegrain mustard

4 tbsp low-fat natural (unsweetened) yogurt

fresh basil leaves

salt and pepper

1 Cut the cheese into 12 sticks, 6.5 cm/2½ inches long. Remove the fat from the ham and slice the meat into 12 strips. Carefully wrap a strip of ham around each stick of cheese and arrange neatly on a serving platter.

2 Halve the artichoke hearts and cut the figs into quarters. Arrange them on the serving platter in groups.

3 Peel the mango, then slice it down each side of the large, flat central stone. Slice the flesh into strips and arrange them so that they form a fan shape on the serving platter.

4 To make the dressing, pare the rind from half of the orange using a vegetable peeler. Cut the rind into small strips and place them in a bowl. Extract the juice from the orange and add it to the bowl containing the rind.

5 Add the passata (sieved tomatoes), mustard, yogurt and seasoning to the bowl and mix together. Shred the basil leaves and mix them into the dressing.

6 Spoon the dressing into a small dish and serve with the Italian Platter, accompanied with bread sticks.

VARIATION

For a change, serve with a French stick or an Italian bread, widely available from supermarkets, and use to mop up the delicious dressing.

Parsley, Chicken & Ham Pâté

Pâté is easy to make at home, and this combination of lean chicken and ham mixed with herbs is especially straightforward.

NUTRITIONAL INFORMATION

Calories 119	Sugars 2g
Protein 20g	Fat 3g
Carbohydrate 2g	Saturates 1g

 55 MINS   0 MINS

SERVES 4

I N G R E D I E N T S

225 g/8 oz lean, skinless chicken, cooked

100 g/3½ oz lean ham, trimmed

small bunch fresh parsley

1 tsp lime rind, grated

2 tbsp lime juice

1 garlic clove, peeled

125 ml/4 fl oz/½ cup low-fat natural fromage frais (unsweetened yogurt)

salt and pepper

1 tsp lime zest, to garnish

TO SERVE

wedges of lime

crisp bread

green salad

VARIATION

This pâté can be made successfully with other kinds of minced, lean, cooked meat such as turkey, beef and pork. Alternatively, replace the meat with peeled prawns (shrimp) and/or white crab meat, or with canned tuna in brine, drained.

1 Dice the chicken and ham and place in a blender or food processor.

2 Add the parsley, lime rind and juice, and garlic to the chicken and ham, and process well until finely minced. Alternatively, finely chop the chicken, ham, parsley and garlic and place in a bowl. Mix gently with the lime rind and juice.

3 Transfer the mixture to a bowl and mix in the fromage frais (yogurt). Season with salt and pepper to taste, cover and leave to chill in the refrigerator for about 30 minutes.

4 Pile the pâté into individual serving dishes and garnish with lime zest. Serve the pâtés with lime wedges, crisp bread and a fresh green salad.

Minted Onion Bhajis

Gram flour (also known as besan flour) is a fine yellow flour made from chickpeas and is available from supermarkets and Asian food shops.

NUTRITIONAL INFORMATION

Calories	.251	Sugars	.7g
Protein	.7g	Fat	.8g
Carbohydrate	.39g	Saturates	.1g

 5 MINS   15 MINS

MAKES 12

I N G R E D I E N T S

125 g/4½ oz/1 cup gram flour

¼ tsp cayenne pepper

¼–½ tsp ground coriander (cilantro)

¼–½ tsp ground cumin

1 tbsp chopped fresh mint

4 tbsp strained thick low-fat yogurt

65 ml/2½ fl oz/¼ cup cold water

1 large onion, quartered and thinly sliced

vegetable oil, for frying

salt and pepper

sprigs of mint, to garnish

1 Put the gram flour into a bowl, add the cayenne pepper, coriander (cilantro), cumin and mint and season with salt and pepper to taste. Stir in the yogurt, water and sliced onion and mix well together.

2 One-third fill a large, deep frying pan with oil and heat until very hot. Drop heaped spoonfuls of the mixture, a few at a time, into the hot oil and use two forks to neaten the mixture into rough ball-shapes.

3 Fry the bhajis until golden brown and cooked through, turning frequently.

4 Drain the bhajis on absorbent kitchen paper (paper towels) and keep warm while cooking the remainder in the same way.

5 Arrange the bhajis on a platter and garnish with sprigs of fresh mint. Serve hot or warm.

COOK'S TIP

Gram flour is excellent for making batter and is used in India in place of flour. It can be made from ground split peas as well as chickpeas (garbanzo beans).

Vegetables with Tahini Dip

This tasty dip is great for livening-up simply-cooked vegetables.
You can vary the vegetables according to the season.

NUTRITIONAL INFORMATION

Calories ....126 Sugars 7g
Protein ....11g Fat 6g
Carbohydrate ....8g Saturates 1g

5 MINS 20 MINS

SERVES 4

INGREDIENTS

225 g/8 oz small broccoli florets

225 g/8 oz small cauliflower florets

225 g/8 oz asparagus, sliced into 5 cm/
2 inch lengths

2 small red onions, quartered

1 tbsp lime juice

2 tsp toasted sesame seeds

1 tbsp chopped fresh chives, to garnish

HOT TAHINI & GARLIC DIP

1 tsp sunflower oil

2 garlic cloves, crushed

½–1 tsp chilli powder

2 tsp tahini (sesame seed paste)

150 ml/¼ pint/⅔ cup low-fat natural
fromage frais

2 tbsp chopped fresh chives

salt and pepper

1 Line the base of a steamer with baking parchment and arrange the vegetables on top.

2 Bring a wok or large saucepan of water to the boil, and place the steamer on top. Sprinkle with lime juice and steam for 10 minutes.

3 To make the hot tahini & garlic dip, heat the sunflower oil in a small non-stick saucepan, add the garlic, chilli powder and seasoning to taste and fry gently for 2–3 minutes until the garlic is softened.

4 Remove the saucepan from the heat and stir in the tahini (sesame seed paste) and fromage frais. Return to the heat and cook gently for 1–2 minutes without boiling. Stir in the chives.

5 Remove the vegetables from the steamer and place on a warmed serving platter. Sprinkle with the sesame seeds and garnish with chopped chives. Serve with the hot dip.

Bruschetta

Traditionally, this Italian savoury is enriched with olive oil. Here, sun-dried tomatoes are a good substitute and only a little oil is used.

NUTRITIONAL INFORMATION

Calories	178	Sugars	.........2g
Protein	.........8g	Fat	...........6g
Carbohydrate	...24g	Saturates	......2g

45 MINS   5 MINS

SERVES 4

I N G R E D I E N T S

60 g/2 oz/¼ cup dry-pack sun-dried tomatoes

300 ml/½ pint/1¼ cups boiling water

35 cm/14 inch long Granary or wholemeal (whole wheat) stick of French bread

1 large garlic clove, halved

25 g/1 oz/¼ cup pitted black olives in brine, drained and quartered

2 tsp olive oil

2 tbsp chopped fresh basil

40 g/1½ oz/⅓ cup grated low-fat Italian Mozzarella cheese

salt and pepper

fresh basil leaves, to garnish

1 Place the sun-dried tomatoes in a heatproof bowl and pour over the boiling water.

2 Set aside for 30 minutes to soften. Drain well and pat dry with paper towels. Slice into thin strips and set aside.

3 Trim and discard the ends from the bread and cut into 12 slices. Arrange on a grill (broiler) rack and place under a preheated hot grill (broiler) and cook for 1–2 minutes on each side until lightly golden.

4 Rub both sides of each piece of bread with the cut sides of the garlic. Top with strips of sun-dried tomato and olives.

5 Brush lightly with olive oil and season well. Sprinkle with the basil and Mozzarella cheese and return to the grill (broiler) for 1–2 minutes until the cheese is melted and bubbling.

6 Transfer to a warmed serving platter and garnish with fresh basil leaves.

COOK'S TIP

If you use sun-dried tomatoes packed in oil, drain them, rinse well in warm water and drain again on kitchen paper (paper towels) to remove as much oil as possible. Sun-dried tomatoes give a rich, full flavour to this dish, but thinly-sliced fresh tomatoes can be used instead.

Cheesy Ham Savoury

Lean ham wrapped around crisp celery, topped with a light crust of cheese and spring onions (scallions), makes a delicious light lunch.

NUTRITIONAL INFORMATION

Calories 188   Sugars 5g
Protein ....15g   Fat 12g
Carbohydrate ....5g   Saturates 7g

  10 MINS   10 MINS

SERVES 4

INGREDIENTS

4 sticks celery, with leaves

12 thin slices of lean ham

1 bunch spring onions (scallions)

175 g/6 oz low-fat soft cheese with garlic and herbs

6 tbsp low-fat natural (unsweetened) yogurt

4 tbsp Parmesan cheese, freshly grated

celery salt and pepper

TO SERVE

tomato salad

crusty bread

1 Wash the celery, remove the leaves and reserve (if wished). Slice each celery stick into 3 equal portions.

2 Cut any visible fat off the ham and lay the slices on a chopping board. Place a piece of celery on each piece of ham and roll up. Place 3 ham and celery rolls in each of 4 small, heatproof dishes.

3 Trim the spring onions (scallions), then finely shred both the white and green parts. Sprinkle the spring onions (scallions) over the ham and celery rolls and season with celery salt and pepper.

4 Mix the soft cheese and yogurt and spoon over the ham and celery rolls.

5 Preheat the grill (broiler) to medium. Sprinkle each portion with 1 tbsp grated Parmesan cheese and grill for 6–7 minutes until hot and the cheese has formed a crust. If the cheese starts to brown too quickly, lower the grill (broiler) setting slightly.

6 Garnish with celery leaves (if using) and serve with a tomato salad and crusty bread.

COOK'S TIP

Parmesan is useful in low-fat recipes because its intense flavour means you need to use only a small amount.

Spicy Chickpea Snack

You can use fresh chickpeas (garbanzo beans), soaked overnight, for this popular Indian snack, but the canned variety is just as flavoursome.

NUTRITIONAL INFORMATION

Calories 190	Sugars 4g	
Protein 9g	Fat 3g	
Carbohydrate ...34g	Saturates 0.3g	

 5 MINS   10 MINS

SERVES 4

INGREDIENTS

400 g/14 oz can chickpeas (garbanzo beans), drained

2 medium potatoes

1 medium onion

2 tbsp tamarind paste

6 tbsp water

1 tsp chilli powder

2 tsp sugar

1 tsp salt

TO GARNISH

1 tomato, sliced

2 fresh green chillies, chopped

fresh coriander (cilantro) leaves

1 Place the chickpeas (garbanzo beans) in a bowl.

COOK'S TIP

Chickpeas (garbanzo beans) have a nutty flavour and slightly crunchy texture. Indian cooks also grind these to make a flour called gram or besan, which is used to make breads, thicken sauces, and to make batters for deep-fried dishes.

2 Using a sharp knife, cut the potatoes into dice.

3 Place the potatoes in a saucepan of water and boil until cooked through. Test by inserting the tip of a knife into the potatoes – they should feel soft and tender. Set the potatoes aside.

4 Using a sharp knife, finely chop the onion. Set aside until required.

5 Mix together the tamarind paste and water. Add the chilli powder, sugar and salt and mix again. Pour the mixture over the chickpeas (garbanzo beans).

6 Add the onion and the diced potatoes, and stir to mix. Season to taste.

7 Transfer to a serving bowl and garnish with tomatoes, chillies and coriander (cilantro) leaves.

Crêpes with Curried Crab

Home-made crêpes are delicious – here, white crab meat is lightly flavoured with curry spices and tossed in a low-fat dressing.

NUTRITIONAL INFORMATION

Calories 279	Sugars 9g
Protein 25g	Fat 7g
Carbohydrate ...31g	Saturates 1g

40 MINS   25 MINS

SERVES 4

INGREDIENTS

115 g/4 oz buckwheat flour

1 large egg, beaten

300 ml/½ pint/1¼ cups skimmed milk

125 g/4½ oz frozen spinach, thawed, well-drained and chopped

2 tsp vegetable oil

FILLING

350 g/12 oz white crab meat

1 tsp mild curry powder

1 tbsp mango chutney

1 tbsp reduced-calorie mayonnaise

2 tbsp low-fat natural (unsweetened) yogurt

2 tbsp fresh coriander (cilantro), chopped

TO SERVE

green salad

lemon wedges

1 Sift the flour into a bowl and remove any husks that remain in the sieve (strainer). Make a well in the centre of the flour and add the egg. Whisk in the milk, then blend in the spinach. Transfer to a jug and leave for 30 minutes.

2 To make the filling, mix together all the ingredients, except the coriander (cilantro), in a bowl, cover and chill until required. Whisk the batter. Brush a small crêpe pan with a little oil, heat until hot and pour in enough batter to cover the base thinly. Cook for 1–2 minutes, turn over and cook for 1 minute until golden. Repeat to make 8 pancakes, layering them on a plate with baking parchment.

3 Stir the coriander (cilantro) into the crab mixture. Fold each pancake into quarters. Open one fold and fill with the crab mixture. Serve warm, with a green salad and lemon wedges.

VARIATION

Try lean diced chicken in a light white sauce or peeled prawns (shrimp) instead of the crab.

Cranberry Turkey Burgers

This recipe is bound to be popular with children and is easy to prepare for their supper or tea.

NUTRITIONAL INFORMATION

Calories	209	Sugars	........15g
Protein	........22g	Fat	...........5g
Carbohydrate	...21g	Saturates	......1g

45 MINS   25 MINS

SERVES 4

I N G R E D I E N T S

350 g/12 oz/1½ cups lean minced (ground) turkey

1 onion, chopped finely

1 tbsp chopped fresh sage

6 tbsp dry white breadcrumbs

4 tbsp cranberry sauce

1 egg white, size 2, lightly beaten

2 tsp sunflower oil

salt and pepper

TO SERVE

4 toasted granary or wholemeal (whole wheat) burger buns

½ lettuce, shredded

4 tomatoes, sliced

4 tsp cranberry sauce

1 Mix together the turkey, onion, sage, seasoning, breadcrumbs and cranberry sauce, then bind with egg white.

2 Press into 4 x 10 cm/4 inch rounds, about 2 cm/¾ inch thick. Chill the burgers for 30 minutes.

3 Line a grill (broiler) rack with baking parchment, making sure the ends are secured underneath the rack to ensure they don't catch fire. Place the burgers on top and brush lightly with oil. Put under a preheated moderate grill (broiler) and cook for 10 minutes. Turn the burgers over, brush again with oil. Cook for a further 12–15 minutes until cooked through.

4 Fill the burger rolls with lettuce, tomato and a burger, and top with cranberry sauce.

COOK'S TIP

Look out for a variety of ready minced (ground) meats at your butchers or supermarket. If unavailable, you can mince (grind) your own by choosing lean cuts and processing them in a blender or food processor.

Stuffed Mushrooms

Large mushrooms have more flavour than the smaller button mushrooms. Serve these mushrooms as a side vegetable or appetizer.

NUTRITIONAL INFORMATION

Calories ....148 Sugars 1g
Protein ....11g Fat 7g
Carbohydrate ....11g Saturates 3g

10 MINS   15 MINS

SERVES 4

INGREDIENTS

12 open-cap mushrooms

4 spring onions (scallions), chopped

4 tsp olive oil

100 g/3½ oz fresh brown breadcrumbs

1 tsp fresh oregano, chopped

100 g/3½ oz low-fat mature (sharp) Cheddar cheese

1 Wash the mushrooms and pat dry with kitchen paper (paper towels). Remove the stalks and chop the stalks finely.

2 Sauté the mushroom stalks and spring onions (scallions) in half of the oil.

3 In a large bowl, mix together the mushroom stalks and spring onions (scallions).

4 Add the breadcrumbs and oregano to the mushrooms and spring onions (scallions), mix and set aside.

5 Crumble the cheese into small pieces in a small bowl. Add the cheese to the breadcrumb mixture and mix well. Spoon the stuffing mixture into the mushroom caps.

6 Drizzle the remaining oil over the mushrooms. Barbecue (grill) on an oiled rack over medium hot coals for 10 minutes or until cooked through.

7 Transfer the mushrooms to serving plates and serve hot.

VARIATION

For a change replace the cheese with finely-chopped chorizo sausage (remove the skin first), chopped hard-boiled eggs, chopped olives or chopped anchovy fillets. Mop up the juices with some crusty bread.

Pasta Provençale

A combination of Italian vegetables tossed in a tomato dressing, served on a bed of assorted salad leaves, makes an appetizing meal.

NUTRITIONAL INFORMATION

Calories 197   Sugars 5g
Protein ....10g   Fat 5g
Carbohydrate ...30g   Saturates 1g

  10 MINS   15 MINS

SERVES 4

I N G R E D I E N T S

225 g/8 oz penne (quills)

1 tbsp olive oil

25 g/1 oz pitted black olives, drained and chopped

25 g/1 oz dry-pack sun-dried tomatoes, soaked, drained and chopped

400 g/14 oz can artichoke hearts, drained and halved

115 g/4 oz baby courgettes (zucchini), trimmed and sliced

115 g/4 oz baby plum tomatoes, halved

100 g/3½ oz assorted baby salad leaves

salt and pepper

shredded basil leaves, to garnish

DRESSING

4 tbsp passata (sieved tomatoes)

2 tbsp low-fat natural fromage frais (unsweetened yogurt)

1 tbsp unsweetened orange juice

1 small bunch fresh basil, shredded

1 Cook the penne (quills) according to the instructions on the packet. Do not overcook the pasta – it should still have 'bite'. Drain well and return to the pan.

2 Stir in the olive oil, salt and pepper, olives and sun-dried tomatoes. Leave to cool.

3 Gently mix the artichokes, courgettes (zucchini) and plum tomatoes into the cooked pasta. Arrange the salad leaves in a serving bowl.

4 To make the dressing, mix all the ingredients together and toss into the vegetables and pasta.

5 Spoon the mixture on top of the salad leaves and garnish with shredded basil leaves.

Lamb & Tomato Koftas

These little meatballs, served with a minty yogurt dressing, can be prepared well in advance, ready to cook when required.

NUTRITIONAL INFORMATION

Calories 183   Sugars 5g
Protein ....15g   Fat 11g
Carbohydrate ....5g   Saturates 4g

15 MINS   10 MINS

SERVES 4

INGREDIENTS

225 g/8 oz finely minced lean lamb

1½ onions, peeled

1-2 garlic cloves, peeled and crushed

1 dried red chilli, finely chopped (optional)

2-3 tsp garam masala

2 tbsp chopped fresh mint

2 tsp lemon juice

salt

2 tbsp vegetable oil

4 small tomatoes, quartered

mint sprigs, to garnish

YOGURT DRESSING

150 ml/¼ pint/⅔ cup low-fat yogurt

5 cm/2 inch piece cucumber, grated

2 tbsp chopped fresh mint

½ tsp toasted cumin seeds (optional)

1 Place the minced lamb in a bowl. Finely chop 1 onion and add to the bowl with the garlic and chilli (if using). Stir in the garam masala, mint and lemon juice and season well with salt. Mix well.

2 Divide the mixture in half, then divide each half into 10 equal portions and form each into a small ball. Roll balls in the oil to coat. Quarter the remaining onion half and separate into layers.

3 Thread 5 of the spicy meatballs, 4 tomato quarters and some of the onion layers on to each of 4 pre-soaked bamboo or metal skewers.

4 Brush the vegetables with the remaining oil and cook the koftas under a hot grill for about 10 minutes, turning frequently until they are browned all over and cooked through.

5 Meanwhile, prepare the yogurt dressing for the koftas. In a small bowl mix together the yogurt, grated cucumber, mint and toasted cumin seeds (if using).

6 Garnish the lamb and tomato koftas with mint sprigs and place on a large serving platter. Serve the koftas hot with the yogurt dressing.

Cheese & Chive Scones

These tea-time classics have been given a healthy twist by the use of low-fat soft cheese and reduced-fat Cheddar cheese.

NUTRITIONAL INFORMATION

Calories 297   Sugars 3g
Protein ....13g   Fat 7g
Carbohydrate ...49g   Saturates 4g

10 MINS   20 MINS

MAKES 10

INGREDIENTS

225 g/8 oz self-raising flour

1 tsp powdered mustard

½ tsp cayenne pepper

½ tsp salt

100 g/3½ oz low-fat soft cheese with added herbs

2 tbsp fresh snipped chives, plus extra to garnish

100 ml/3½ fl oz and 2 tbsp skimmed milk

60 g/2 oz reduced-fat mature (sharp) Cheddar cheese, grated

low-fat soft cheese, to serve

1 Preheat the oven to 200°C/400°F/Gas Mark 6. Sift the flour, mustard, cayenne and salt into a mixing bowl.

2 Add the soft cheese to the mixture and mix together until well incorporated. Stir in the snipped chives.

3 Make a well in the centre of the ingredients and gradually pour in 100 ml/3½ fl oz milk, stirring as you pour, until the mixture forms a soft dough.

4 Turn the dough on to a floured surface and knead lightly. Roll out until 2 cm/¾ inch thick and use a 5 cm/2 inch plain pastry cutter to stamp out as many rounds as you can. Transfer the rounds to a baking sheet.

5 Re-knead the dough trimmings together and roll out again. Stamp out more rounds – you should be able to make 10 scones in total.

6 Brush the scones with the remaining milk and sprinkle with the grated cheese. Bake in the oven for 15–20 minutes until risen and golden. Transfer to a wire rack to cool. Serve warm with low-fat soft cheese, garnished with chives.

VARIATION

For sweet scones, omit the mustard, cayenne pepper, chives and grated cheese. Replace the flavoured soft cheese with plain low-fat soft cheese. Add 75 g/2¾ oz currants and 25 g/ 1 oz caster (superfine) sugar. Serve with low-fat soft cheese and fruit spread.

Oat-Crusted Chicken Pieces

A very low-fat chicken recipe with a refreshingly light, mustard-spiced sauce, which is ideal for a healthy lunchbox or a light meal with salad.

NUTRITIONAL INFORMATION

Calories	120	Sugars	.........3g
Protein	........15g	Fat	...........3g
Carbohydrate	....8g	Saturates	......1g

 5 MINS   40 MINS

SERVES 4

I N G R E D I E N T S

25 g/1 oz/⅓ cup rolled oats

1 tbsp chopped fresh rosemary

4 skinless chicken quarters

1 egg white

150 g/5½ oz/½ cup natural low-fat fromage frais

2 tsp wholegrain mustard

salt and pepper

grated carrot salad, to serve

1 Mix together the rolled oats, chopped fresh rosemary and salt and pepper.

2 Brush each piece of chicken evenly with egg white, then coat in the oat mixture.

3 Place the chicken pieces on a baking tray (cookie sheet) and bake in a preheated oven, 200°C/400°F/Gas Mark 6, for about 40 minutes. Test to see if the chicken is cooked by inserting a skewer into the thickest part of the chicken – the juices should run clear without a trace of pink.

4 Mix together the fromage frais and mustard, season with salt and pepper to taste.

5 Serve the chicken, hot or cold, with the sauce and a grated carrot salad.

Hot Pot Chops

A Hot Pot is a lamb casserole, made with carrots and onions and with a potato topping. The chops used here are an interesting alternative.

NUTRITIONAL INFORMATION

Calories 250	Sugars 2g	
Protein 27g	Fat 12g	
Carbohydrate 8g	Saturates 5g	

10 MINS   30 MINS

SERVES 4

I N G R E D I E N T S

4 lean, boneless lamb leg steaks, about
   125 g/4½ oz each

1 small onion, thinly sliced

1 medium carrot, thinly sliced

1 medium potato, thinly sliced

1 tsp olive oil

1 tsp dried rosemary

salt and pepper

fresh rosemary, to garnish

freshly steamed green vegetables,
   to serve

1 Preheat the oven to 180°C/350°F/Gas Mark 4. Using a sharp knife, trim any excess fat from the lamb steaks.

2 Season both sides of the steaks with salt and pepper and arrange them on a baking tray.

3 Alternate layers of sliced onion, carrot and potato on top of each lamb steak.

4 Brush the tops of the potato lightly with oil, season well with salt and pepper to taste and then sprinkle with a little dried rosemary.

5 Bake the hot pot chops in the oven for 25–30 minutes until the lamb is tender and cooked through.

6 Drain the lamb on absorbent kitchen paper (paper towels) and transfer to a warmed serving plate.

7 Garnish with fresh rosemary and serve accompanied with a selection of green vegetables.

VARIATION

This recipe would work equally well with boneless chicken breasts. Pound the chicken slightly with a meat mallet or covered rolling pin so that the pieces are the same thickness throughout.

Kibbeh

This Lebanese barbeque dish is similar to the Turkish kofte and the Indian kofta, but the spices used to flavour the meat are quite different.

NUTRITIONAL INFORMATION

Calories 232	Sugars 3g
Protein 19g	Fat 13g
Carbohydrate 9g	Saturates 4g

1 HOUR   15 MINS

SERVES 4

I N G R E D I E N T S

75 g/2¾ oz couscous

1 small onion

350 g/12 oz lean minced lamb

½ tsp ground cinnamon

¼ tsp cayenne

4 tsp ground allspice

green salad and onion rings, to serve

B A S T E

2 tbsp tomato ketchup (catsup)

2 tbsp sunflower oil

1 Place the couscous in a large bowl, cover with cold water and leave to stand for 30 minutes or until the couscous has swelled and softened. Alternatively, soak the couscous according to the instructions on the packet.

2 Drain the couscous through a sieve and squeeze out as much moisture as you can.

3 If you have a food processor, add the onion and chop finely. Add the lamb and process briefly to chop the mince further. If you do not have a processor, grate the onion then add to the lamb.

4 Combine the couscous, lamb and spices and mix well together. Divide the mixture into 8 equal sized portions. Press and shape the mixture around 8 skewers, pressing the mixture together firmly so that it holds it shape. Leave to chill for at least 30 minutes or until required.

5 To make the baste, combine the oil and ketchup (catsup).

6 Barbecue (grill) the kibbeh over hot coals for 10–15 minutes, turning and basting frequently. Serve with barbecued (grilled) onion rings and green salad leaves.

Lamb with a Spice Crust

Lamb neck fillet is a tender cut that is not too thick and is, therefore, ideal for cooking on the barbecue (grill).

NUTRITIONAL INFORMATION

Calories 203	Sugars 9g
Protein 16g	Fat 10g
Carbohydrate . . .12g	Saturates 4g

 5 MINS   45 MINS

SERVES 4

I N G R E D I E N T S

1 tbsp olive oil

2 tbsp light muscovado sugar

2 tbsp wholegrain mustard

1 tbsp horseradish sauce

1 tbsp plain (all-purpose) flour

350 g/12 oz neck fillet of lamb

salt and pepper

T O   S E R V E

coleslaw

slices of tomato

1 Combine the oil, sugar, mustard, horseradish sauce, flour and salt and pepper to taste in a shallow, non-metallic dish until they are well mixed.

2 Roll the lamb in the spice mixture until well coated.

COOK'S TIP

If preferred, the lamb can be completely removed from the kitchen foil for the second part of the cooking. Barbecue (grill) the lamb directly over the coals for a smokier barbecue (grill) flavour, basting with extra oil if necessary.

 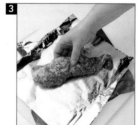 

3 Lightly oil one or two pieces of foil or a large, double thickness of foil. Place the lamb on the foil and wrap it up so that the meat is completely enclosed.

4 Place the foil parcel over hot coals for 30 minutes, turning the parcel over occasionally.

5 Open the kitchen foil, spoon the cooking juices over the lamb and continue to barbecue (grill) for a further 10-15 minutes or until cooked through.

6 Place the lamb on a platter and remove the foil. Cut into thick slices and serve with coleslaw and tomato slices.

Pork & Apple Skewers

Flavoured with mustard and served with a mustard sauce, these kebabs make an ideal lunch.

NUTRITIONAL INFORMATION

Calories 290	Sugars 11g
Protein 24g	Fat 17g
Carbohydrate 11g	Saturates 5g

10 MINS   15 MINS

SERVES 4

INGREDIENTS

450 g/1 lb pork fillet

2 (dessert) eating apples

a little lemon juice

1 lemon

2 tsp wholegrain mustard

2 tsp Dijon mustard

2 tbsp apple or orange juice

2 tbsp sunflower oil

crusty brown bread, to serve

MUSTARD SAUCE

1 tbsp wholegrain mustard

1 tsp Dijon mustard

6 tbsp single (light) cream

1 To make the mustard sauce, combine the wholegrain and Dijon mustards in a small bowl and slowly blend in the cream. Leave to stand until required.

2 Cut the pork fillet into bite-size pieces and set aside until required.

3 Core the apples, then cut them into thick wedges. Toss the apple wedges in a little lemon juice – this will prevent any discoloration. Slice the lemon.

4 Thread the pork, apple and lemon slices alternately on to 4 metal or pre-soaked wooden skewers.

5 Mix together the mustards, apple or orange juice and sunflower oil. Brush the mixture over the kebabs and barbecue (grill) over hot coals for 10–15 minutes,

until cooked through, frequently turning and basting the kebabs with the mustard marinade.

6 Transfer the kebabs to warm serving plates and spoon over a little of the mustard sauce. Serve the kebabs with fresh, crusty brown bread.

Ginger Beef with Chilli

Serve these fruity, hot and spicy steaks with noodles. Use a non-stick ridged frying pan (skillet) to cook with a minimum of fat.

NUTRITIONAL INFORMATION

Calories	179	Sugars	.........8g
Protein	........21g	Fat	...........6g
Carbohydrate	....8g	Saturates	......2g

40 MINS · 10 MINS

SERVES 4

INGREDIENTS

4 lean beef steaks (such as rump, sirloin or fillet), 100 g/3½ oz each

2 tbsp ginger wine

2.5 cm/1 inch piece root (fresh) ginger, finely chopped

1 garlic clove, crushed

1 tsp ground chilli

1 tsp vegetable oil

salt and pepper

red chilli strips, to garnish

TO SERVE

freshly cooked noodles

2 spring onions (scallions), shredded

RELISH

225 g/8 oz fresh pineapple

1 small red (bell) pepper

1 red chilli

2 tbsp light soy sauce

1 piece stem ginger in syrup, drained and chopped

1 Trim any excess fat from the beef if necessary. Using a meat mallet or covered rolling pin, pound the steaks until 1 cm/½ inch thick. Season on both sides and place in a shallow dish.

2 Mix the ginger wine, root (fresh) ginger, garlic and chilli and pour over the meat. Cover and chill for 30 minutes.

3 Meanwhile, make the relish. Peel and finely chop the pineapple and place it in a bowl. Halve, deseed and finely chop the (bell) pepper and chilli. Stir into the pineapple together with the soy sauce and stem ginger. Cover and chill until required.

4 Brush a grill (broiler) pan with the oil and heat until very hot. Drain the beef and add to the pan, pressing down to seal. Lower the heat and cook for 5 minutes. Turn the steaks over and cook for a further 5 minutes.

5 Drain the steaks on kitchen paper and transfer to serving plates. Garnish with chilli strips, and serve with noodles, spring onions (scallions) and the relish.

Meatball Brochettes

Children will love these tasty meatballs on a skewer, which are economical and easy to make on the barbecue (grill).

NUTRITIONAL INFORMATION

Calories . . . . . . .120 Sugars 2g
Protein . . . . .17g Fat 5g
Carbohydrate . . . .2g Saturates 2g

1 HOUR   10 MINS

SERVES 4

I N G R E D I E N T S

25 g/1 oz cracked wheat

350 g/12 oz lean minced beef

1 onion, chopped very finely (optional)

1 tbsp tomato ketchup (catsup)

1 tbsp brown fruity sauce

1 tbsp chopped, fresh parsley

beaten egg, to bind

8 cherry tomatoes

8 button mushrooms

oil, to baste

8 bread finger rolls, to serve

1 Place the cracked wheat in a bowl and cover with boiling water. Leave to soak for 20 minutes or until softened. Drain thoroughly and leave to cool.

2 Place the soaked wheat, minced beef, onion (if using), ketchup (catsup), brown fruity sauce and chopped fresh parsley together in a mixing bowl and mix well until all the ingredients are well combined. Add a little beaten egg if necessary to bind the mixture together.

3 Using your hands, shape the meat mixture into 18 even-sized balls. Leave to chill in the refrigerator for 30 minutes.

4 Thread the meatballs on to 8 pre-soaked wooden skewers, alternating them with the cherry tomatoes and button mushrooms.

5 Brush the brochettes with a little oil and barbecue (grill) over hot coals for about 10 minutes, until cooked through, turning occasionally and brushing with a little more oil if the meat starts to dry out.

6 Transfer the meatball brochettes to warm serving plates. Cut open the bread finger rolls and push the meat and vegetables off the skewer into the open rolls, using a fork. Serve immediately.

Pork with Ratatouille Sauce

Serve this delicious combination of meat and vegetables with baked potatoes for an appetizing supper dish.

NUTRITIONAL INFORMATION

Calories	230	Sugars	.........8g
Protein	........29g	Fat	...........9g
Carbohydrate	....8g	Saturates	......3g

10 MINS   35 MINS

SERVES 4

INGREDIENTS

4 lean, boneless pork chops, about
   125 g/4½ oz each

1 tsp dried mixed herbs

salt and pepper

baked potatoes, to serve

SAUCE

1 medium onion

1 garlic clove

1 small green (bell) pepper, deseeded

1 small yellow (bell) pepper, deseeded

1 medium courgette (zucchini), trimmed

100 g/3½ oz button mushrooms

400 g/14 oz can chopped tomatoes

2 tbsp tomato purée (paste)

1 tsp dried mixed herbs

1 tsp caster (superfine) sugar

COOK'S TIP

This vegetable sauce could
be served with any other grilled
(broiled) or baked meat or fish.
It would also make an excellent
alternative filling for
savoury crêpes.

  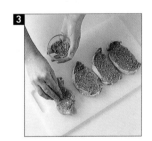

1 To make the sauce, peel and chop the onion and garlic. Dice the (bell) peppers. Dice the courgette (zucchini). Wipe and halve the mushrooms.

2 Place all of the vegetables in a saucepan and stir in the chopped tomatoes and tomato purée (paste). Add the dried herbs, sugar and plenty of seasoning. Bring to the boil, cover and simmer for 20 minutes.

3 Meanwhile, preheat the grill (broiler) to medium. Trim away any excess fat from the chops, then season on both sides and rub in the dried mixed herbs. Cook the chops for 5 minutes, then turn over and cook for a further 6–7 minutes or until cooked through.

4 Drain the chops on absorbent kitchen paper and serve accompanied with the sauce and baked potatoes.

Sweet Lamb Fillet

Lamb fillet, enhanced by a sweet and spicy glaze, is cooked on the barbecue (grill) in a kitchen foil parcel for deliciously moist results.

NUTRITIONAL INFORMATION

Calories	258	Sugars	........13g
Protein	........24g	Fat	..........13g
Carbohydrate	...13g	Saturates	......5g

5 MINS   1 HOUR

SERVES 4

I N G R E D I E N T S

2 fillets of neck of lean lamb, each 225 g/8 oz

1 tbsp olive oil

½ onion, chopped finely

1 clove garlic, crushed

2.5 cm/1 inch piece root (fresh) ginger, grated

5 tbsp apple juice

3 tbsp smooth apple sauce

1 tbsp light muscovado sugar

1 tbsp tomato ketchup (catsup)

½ tsp mild mustard

salt and pepper

green salad leaves, croûtons and fresh crusty bread, to serve

1 Place the lamb fillet on a large piece of double thickness kitchen foil. Season with salt and pepper to taste.

2 Heat the oil in a small pan and fry the onion and garlic for 2–3 minutes until softened but not browned. Stir in the grated ginger and cook for 1 minute, stirring occasionally.

3 Stir in the apple juice, apple sauce, sugar, ketchup (catsup) and mustard and bring to the boil. Boil rapidly for about 10 minutes until reduced by half.

Stir the mixture occasionally so that it does not burn and stick to the base of the pan.

4 Brush half of the sauce over the lamb, then wrap up the lamb in the kitchen foil to completely enclose it. Barbecue (grill) the lamb parcels over hot coals for about 25 minutes, turning the parcel over occasionally.

5 Open out the kitchen foil and brush the lamb with some of the sauce. Continue to barbecue (grill) for a further 15–20 minutes or until cooked through.

6 Place the lamb on a chopping board, remove the foil and cut into thick slices. Transfer to serving plates and spoon over the remaining sauce. Serve with green salad leaves, croûtons and fresh crusty bread.

Pan-Fried Liver with Thyme

This elegant dish is very simple to make. You can use either calf's or lamb's liver for the main ingredient.

NUTRITIONAL INFORMATION

Calories 462	Sugars 1g
Protein 27g	Fat 31g
Carbohydrate . . .14g	Saturates 6g

🥧 5 MINS   🕐 10 MINS

SERVES 1

INGREDIENTS

1 slice calf's liver, about 125 g/4½ oz, or 2 smaller slices, or 2 slices lamb's liver

1 tbsp seasoned flour

2 tsp oil

15 g/½ oz/1 tbsp butter or margarine

2 tbsp white wine

½ tsp chopped fresh thyme or a large pinch of dried thyme

pinch of finely grated lime or lemon rind

2 tsp lemon juice

1 tsp capers

1–2 tbsp double (heavy) cream (optional)

salt and pepper

TO GARNISH

lemon or lime slices

fresh thyme or parsley

COOK'S TIP

Liver is traditionally served with bacon and onions. Grilled (broiled) bacon rolls and crisply fried onions can be used as an extra garnish, if desired.

1 Trim the liver if necessary and toss in the seasoned flour until evenly coated.

2 Heat the oil and margarine in a frying pan (skillet). When foaming, add the liver and fry for 2–3 minutes on each side until well sealed and just cooked through. Take care not to overcook or the liver will become tough and hard. Transfer to a plate and keep warm.

3 Add the wine, 1 tablespoon of water, the thyme, citrus rind, lemon juice, capers and seasoning to the pan juices, and heat through gently until bubbling and syrupy. Add the cream (if using) to the sauce and reheat gently. Adjust the seasoning and spoon over the liver.

4 Serve the liver, garnished with lemon or lime slices and thyme or parsley, with new potatoes and a salad.

Minty Lamb Kebabs

These spicy lamb kebabs go well with the cool cucumber and yogurt dip.
In the summer you can barbecue (grill) the kebabs outside.

NUTRITIONAL INFORMATION

Calories 295   Sugars 4g
Protein . . . . .29g   Fat 18g
Carbohydrate . . . .4g   Saturates 9g

5 MINS   20 MINS

SERVES 4

INGREDIENTS

2 tsp coriander seeds

2 tsp cumin seeds

3 cloves

3 green cardamom pods

6 black peppercorns

1 cm/½ inch piece ginger root

2 garlic cloves

2 tbsp chopped fresh mint

1 small onion, chopped

400 g/14 oz/1¾ cups minced (ground) lamb

½ tsp salt

lime slices to serve

DIP

150 ml/5 fl oz/⅔ cup low-fat natural yogurt

2 tbsp chopped fresh mint

7 cm/3 inch piece of cucumber, grated

1 tsp mango chutney

1 Heat a frying pan (skillet) and dry-fry the coriander, cumin, cloves, cardamom pods and peppercorns until they turn a shade darker and release a roasted aroma.

2 Grind the spices in a coffee grinder, spice mill or a pestle and mortar.

3 Put the ginger and garlic into a food processor or blender and process to a purée. Add the ground spices, mint, onion, lamb and salt and process until chopped finely. Alternatively, finely chop the garlic and ginger and mix with the ground spices and remaining kebab ingredients.

4 Mould the kebab mixture into small sausage shapes on 4 kebab skewers.

Cook under a preheated hot grill (broiler) for 10–15 minutes, turning the skewers occasionally.

5 To make the dip, mix together the yogurt, mint, cucumber and mango chutney.

6 Serve the kebabs with lime slices and the dip.

Tangy Pork Fillet

Barbecued (grilled) in a parcel of kitchen foil, these tasty pork fillets are served with a tangy orange sauce.

NUTRITIONAL INFORMATION

Calories 230	Sugars 16g
Protein 19g	Fat 9g
Carbohydrate . . .20g	Saturates 3g

🥧🥧

🍞 10 MINS   🕐 55 MINS

SERVES 4

INGREDIENTS

400 g/14 oz lean pork fillet

3 tbsp orange marmalade

grated rind and juice of 1 orange

1 tbsp white wine vinegar

dash of Tabasco sauce

salt and pepper

SAUCE

1 tbsp olive oil

1 small onion, chopped

1 small green (bell) pepper, deseeded and
thinly sliced

1 tbsp cornflour (cornstarch)

150 ml/5 fl oz/⅔ cup orange juice

TO SERVE

cooked rice

mixed salad leaves

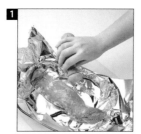

1 Place a large piece of double thickness foil in a shallow dish. Put the pork fillet in the centre of the foil and season.

2 Heat the marmalade, orange rind and juice, vinegar and Tabasco sauce in a small pan, stirring until the marmalade melts and the ingredients combine. Pour the mixture over the pork and wrap the meat in foil, making sure that the parcel is well sealed so that the juices cannot run out. Place over hot coals and barbecue (grill) for about 25 minutes, turning the parcel occasionally.

3 For the sauce, heat the oil and cook the onion for 2–3 minutes. Add the (bell) pepper and cook for 3–4 minutes.

4 Remove the pork from the kitchen foil and place on to the rack. Pour the juices into the pan with the sauce.

5 Barbecue (grill) the pork for a further 10–20 minutes, turning, until cooked through and golden on the outside.

6 In a small bowl, mix the cornflour (cornstarch) with a little orange juice to form a paste. Add to the sauce with the remaining cooking juices. Cook, stirring, until the sauce thickens. Slice the pork, spoon over the sauce and serve with rice and mixed salad leaves.

Teppanyaki

This simple, Japanese style of cooking, is ideal for thinly-sliced breast of chicken. You can use thin turkey escalopes, if you prefer.

NUTRITIONAL INFORMATION

Calories 206	Sugars 4g	
Protein 30g	Fat 7g	
Carbohydrate 6g	Saturates 2g	

5 MINS   10 MINS

SERVES 4

I N G R E D I E N T S

4 boneless chicken breasts

1 red (bell) pepper

1 green (bell) pepper

4 spring onions (scallions)

8 baby corn cobs (corn-on-the-cob)

100 g/3½ oz/½ cup bean sprouts

1 tbsp sesame or sunflower oil

4 tbsp soy sauce

4 tbsp mirin

1 tbsp grated fresh ginger root

1 Remove the skin from the chicken and slice at a slight angle, to a thickness of about 5 mm/¼ inch.

2 Deseed and thinly slice the (bell) peppers and trim and slice the spring onions (scallions) and corn cobs (corn-on-the-cob).

3 Arrange the (bell) peppers, spring onions (scallions), corn and bean sprouts on a plate with the sliced chicken.

4 Heat a large griddle or heavy frying pan then lightly brush with oil. Add the vegetables and chicken slices in small batches, allowing space between them so that they cook thoroughly.

5 Combine the soy sauce, mirin and ginger and serve as a dip with the chicken and vegetables.

COOK'S TIP

Mirin is a rich, sweet rice wine which you can buy in oriental shops, but if it is not available add 1 tablespoon of soft light brown sugar to the sauce instead.

Karahi Chicken

A karahi is an extremely versatile two-handled metal pan, similar to a wok. Food is always cooked over a high heat in a karahi.

NUTRITIONAL INFORMATION

Calories	270	Sugars	.........1g
Protein	........41g	Fat	...........11g
Carbohydrate	....1g	Saturates	......2g

5 MINS   20 MINS

SERVES 4

INGREDIENTS

2 tbsp ghee

3 garlic cloves, crushed

1 onion, chopped finely

2 tbsp garam masala

1 tsp coriander seeds, ground

½ tsp dried mint

1 bay leaf

750 g/1 lb 10 oz lean boneless chicken meat, diced

200 ml/7 fl oz/scant 1 cup chicken stock

1 tbsp fresh coriander (cilantro), chopped

salt

warm naan bread or chapatis, to serve

1 Heat the ghee in a karahi, wok or a large, heavy frying pan (skillet). Add the garlic and onion. Stir-fry for about 4 minutes until the onion is golden.

2 Stir in the garam masala, ground coriander, mint and bay leaf.

3 Add the chicken and cook over a high heat, stirring occasionally, for about 5 minutes. Add the stock and simmer for 10 minutes, until the sauce has thickened and the chicken juices run clear when the meat is tested with a sharp knife.

4 Stir in the fresh coriander (cilantro) and salt to taste, mix well and serve immediately with warm naan bread or chapatis.

COOK'S TIP

Always heat a karahi or wok before you add the oil to help maintain the high temperature.

Lime Chicken Kebabs

These succulent chicken kebabs are coated in a sweet lime dressing and are served with a lime and mango relish. They make an ideal light meal.

NUTRITIONAL INFORMATION

Calories	199	Sugars 14g
Protein	.......28g	Fat 4g
Carbohydrate	...14g	Saturates 1g

15 MINS   10 MINS

SERVES 4

I N G R E D I E N T S

4 lean boneless chicken breasts, skinned, about 125 g/4½ oz each

3 tbsp lime marmalade

1 tsp white wine vinegar

½ tsp lime rind, finely grated

1 tbsp lime juice

salt and pepper

T O S E R V E

lime wedges

boiled white rice, sprinkled with chilli powder

S A L S A

1 small mango

1 small red onion

1 tbsp lime juice

1 tbsp fresh coriander (cilantro), chopped

1 Slice the chicken breasts into thin pieces and thread on to 8 skewers so that the meat forms an S-shape down each skewer.

2 Preheat the grill (broiler) to medium. Arrange the chicken kebabs on the grill (broiler) rack. Mix together the lime marmalade, vinegar, lime rind and juice. Season with salt and pepper to taste. Brush the dressing generously over the chicken and grill (broil) for 5 minutes. Turn the chicken over, brush with the dressing again and grill (broil) for a further 4-5 minutes until the chicken is cooked through.

3 Meanwhile, prepare the salsa. Peel the mango and slice the flesh off the smooth, central stone. Dice the flesh into small pieces and place in a small bowl.

4 Peel and finely chop the onion and mix into the mango, together with the lime juice and chopped coriander (cilantro). Season, cover and chill until required.

5 Serve the chicken kebabs with the salsa, accompanied with wedges of lime and boiled rice sprinkled with chilli powder.

COOK'S TIP

To prevent sticking, lightly oil metal skewers or dip bamboo skewers in water before threading the chicken on to them.

Cajun Chicken Gumbo

This complete main course is cooked in one saucepan. If you're cooking for one, halve the ingredients – the cooking time should stay the same.

NUTRITIONAL INFORMATION

Calories 425	Sugars 8g	
Protein 34g	Fat 12g	
Carbohydrate ...48g	Saturates 3g	

5 MINS   25 MINS

SERVES 2

I N G R E D I E N T S

1 tbsp sunflower oil

4 chicken thighs

1 small onion, diced

2 sticks (stalks) celery, diced

1 small green (bell) pepper, diced

90 g/3 oz/½ cup long grain rice

300 ml/½ pint/1¼ cups chicken stock

1 small red chilli

225 g/8 oz okra

15 ml/1 tbsp tomato purée (paste)

salt and pepper

1 Heat the oil in a wide pan and fry the chicken until golden. Remove the chicken from the pan.

2 Stir in the onion, celery and pepper and fry for 1 minute. Pour off any excess oil.

3 Add the rice and fry, stirring for a further minute. Add the stock and heat until boiling. Thinly slice the chilli and trim the okra. Add to the pan with the tomato purée (paste). Season to taste.

4 Return the chicken to the pan and stir. Cover tightly and simmer gently for 15 minutes, or until the rice is tender, the chicken is thoroughly cooked and the liquid absorbed. Stir occasionally and if it becomes too dry, add a little extra stock.

COOK'S TIP

The whole chilli makes the dish hot and spicy – if you prefer a milder flavour, discard the seeds of the chilli.

Citrus Duckling Skewers

The tartness of citrus fruit goes well with the rich meat of duckling. Duckling makes a change from chicken for the barbecue (grill).

NUTRITIONAL INFORMATION

Calories	205	Sugars	.........5g
Protein	........24g	Fat	..........10g
Carbohydrate	....5g	Saturates	......2g

45 MINS   20 MINS

SERVES 12

I N G R E D I E N T S

3 duckling breasts, skinned, boned and cut into bite-size pieces

1 small red onion, cut into wedges

1 small aubergine (eggplant), cut into cubes

lime and lemon wedges, to garnish (optional)

M A R I N A D E

grated rind and juice of 1 lemon

grated rind and juice of 1 lime

grated rind and juice of 1 orange

1 clove garlic, crushed

1 tsp dried oregano

2 tbsp olive oil

dash of Tabasco sauce

1 Cut the duckling into bite-sized pieces. Place in a non-metallic bowl together with the prepared vegetables.

2 To make the marinade, place the lemon, lime and orange rinds and juices, garlic, oregano, oil and Tabasco sauce in a screw-top jar and shake until well combined. Pour the marinade over the duckling and vegetables and toss to coat. Leave to marinate for 30 minutes.

3 Remove the duckling and vegetables from the marinade and thread them on to skewers, reserving the marinade.

4 Barbecue (grill) the skewers on an oiled rack over medium hot coals, turning and basting frequently with the reserved marinade, for 15-20 minutes until the meat is cooked through. Serve the kebabs garnished with lemon and lime wedges for squeezing (if using).

COOK'S TIP

For more zing add 1 teaspoon of chilli sauce to the marinade. The meat can be marinated for several hours, but it is best to marinate the vegetables separately for only about 30 minutes.

Chicken Jalfrezi

This is a quick and tasty way to use leftover roast chicken. The sauce can also be used for any cooked poultry, lamb or beef.

NUTRITIONAL INFORMATION

Calories 270   Sugars 3g
Protein . . . . .36g   Fat 11g
Carbohydrate . . . .7g   Saturates 2g

25 MINS   15 MINS

SERVES 4

I N G R E D I E N T S

1 tsp mustard oil

3 tbsp vegetable oil

1 large onion, chopped finely

3 garlic cloves, crushed

1 tbsp tomato purée (paste)

2 tomatoes, skinned and chopped

1 tsp ground turmeric

½ tsp cumin seeds, ground

½ tsp coriander seeds, ground

½ tsp chilli powder

½ tsp garam masala

1 tsp red wine vinegar

1 small red (bell) pepper, chopped

125 g/4½ oz/1 cup frozen broad (fava)
    beans

500 g/1 lb 2 oz cooked chicken, cut into
    bite-sized pieces

salt

sprigs of fresh coriander (cilantro),
    to garnish

1 Heat the mustard oil in a large frying pan (skillet) set over a high heat for about 1 minute until it begins to smoke.

2 Add the vegetable oil, reduce the heat and then add the onion and the garlic. Fry the garlic and onion until they are golden.

3 Add the tomato purée (paste), chopped tomatoes, turmeric, ground cumin and coriander seeds, chilli powder, garam masala and wine vinegar to the frying pan (skillet). Stir the mixture until fragrant.

4 Add the red (bell) pepper and broad (fava) beans and stir for 2 minutes until the pepper is softened. Stir in the chicken, and salt to taste.

5 Simmer gently for 6–8 minutes until the chicken is heated through and the beans are tender.

6 Serve garnished with sprigs of coriander (cilantro).

Spiced Apricot Chicken

Spiced chicken legs are partially boned and packed with dried apricot.
A golden, spiced, low-fat yogurt coating keeps the chicken moist.

NUTRITIONAL INFORMATION

Calories	305	Sugars	........21g
Protein	........15g	Fat	...........8g
Carbohydrate	...45g	Saturates	......1g

 10 MINS   40 MINS

SERVES 4

INGREDIENTS

4 large, lean skinless chicken leg quarters

finely grated rind of 1 lemon

200 g/7 oz/1 cup ready-to-eat dried apricots

1 tbsp ground cumin

1 tsp ground turmeric

125 g/4½ oz/½ cup low-fat natural yogurt

salt and pepper

TO SERVE

250 g/9 oz/1½ cups brown rice

2 tbsp flaked hazelnuts, toasted

2 tbsp sunflower seeds, toasted

1 Remove any excess fat from the chicken legs. Use a small sharp knife to carefully cut the flesh away from the thigh bone. Scrape the meat away down as far as the knuckle. Grasp the thigh bone firmly and twist it to break it away from the drumstick.

2 Open out the boned part of the chicken and sprinkle with lemon rind and pepper. Pack the dried apricots into each piece of chicken.

3 Fold over to enclose, and secure with cocktail sticks. Mix together the cumin, turmeric, yogurt and salt and pepper, then brush this mixture over the

chicken to coat evenly. Place the chicken in an ovenproof dish and bake in a preheated oven, 190°C/375°F/Gas Mark 5, for 35–40 minutes, or until the chicken juices run clear, not pink, when pierced through the thickest part with a skewer.

4 Meanwhile, cook the rice in boiling, lightly salted water until just tender, then drain well. Stir the hazelnuts and sunflower seeds into the rice and serve.

VARIATION

For a change use dried herbs instead of spices to flavour the coating. Use dried oregano, tarragon or rosemary – but remember dried herbs are more powerful than fresh, so you will only need a little.

Ginger Chicken & Corn

Chicken wings and corn in a sticky ginger marinade are designed to be eaten with the fingers – there's no other way!

NUTRITIONAL INFORMATION

Calories 123	Sugars 3g
Protein 14g	Fat 6g
Carbohydrate 3g	Saturates 1g

10 MINS   20 MINS

SERVES 6

INGREDIENTS

3 cobs fresh sweetcorn (corn-on-the-cob)

12 chicken wings

2.5cm/1 inch piece fresh ginger root

6 tbsp lemon juice

4 tsp sunflower oil

1 tbsp golden caster (superfine) sugar

jacket potatoes or salad, to serve

1 Remove the husks and silks from the corn. Using a sharp knife, cut each cob into 6 slices.

2 Place the corn in a large bowl with the chicken wings.

3 Peel and grate the ginger root or chop finely. Place in a bowl and add the lemon juice, sunflower oil and golden caster (superfine) sugar. Mix together until well combined.

4 Toss the corn and chicken in the ginger mixture to coat evely.

5 Thread the corn and chicken wings alternately on to metal or pre-soaked wooden skewers, to make turning easier.

6 Cook under a preheated moderately hot grill (broiler) or barbecue (grill) for 15–20 minutes, basting with the gingery glaze and turning frequently until the corn is golden brown and tender and the chicken is cooked. Serve with jacket potatoes or salad.

COOK'S TIP

Cut off the wing tips before grilling (broiling) as they burn very easily. Alternatively, you can cover them with small pieces of foil.

Mexican Chicken

Chilli, tomatoes and corn are typical ingredients in a Mexican dish. This is a quick and easy meal for unexpected guests.

NUTRITIONAL INFORMATION

Calories 207	Sugars 8g
Protein 18g	Fat 9g
Carbohydrate . . .13g	Saturates 2g

5 MINS   35 MINS

SERVES 4

INGREDIENTS

2 tbsp oil

8 chicken drumsticks

1 medium onion, finely chopped

1 tsp chilli powder

1 tsp ground coriander (cilantro)

425 g/15 oz can chopped tomatoes

2 tbsp tomato purée (paste)

125 g/4½ oz/⅔ cup frozen sweetcorn
   (corn-on-the-cob)

salt and pepper

TO SERVE

boiled rice

mixed (bell) pepper salad

1 Heat the oil in a large frying pan (skillet), add the chicken drumsticks and cook over a medium heat until lightly browned on all sides. Remove from the pan and set aside.

2 Add the onion to the pan and cook for 3–4 minutes until soft, then stir in the chilli powder and coriander (cilantro) and cook for a few seconds.

3 Add the chopped tomatoes with their juice and the tomato purée (paste).

4 Return the chicken to the pan and simmer gently for 20 minutes until the chicken is tender and thoroughly cooked. Add the sweetcorn (corn-on-the-cob) and cook a further 3–4 minutes. Season to taste.

5 Serve with boiled rice and mixed (bell) pepper salad.

COOK'S TIP

If you dislike the heat of the chillies, just leave them out – the chicken will still taste delicious.

Prawn (Shrimp) Bhuna

This is a fiery recipe with subtle undertones. As the flavour of the prawns (shrimp) should be noticeable, the spices should not take over.

NUTRITIONAL INFORMATION

Calories 141   Sugars 0.4g
Protein . . . . .19g   Fat 7g
Carbohydrate . . . .1g   Saturates 1g

15 MINS   20 MINS

SERVES 4–6

I N G R E D I E N T S

2 dried red chillies, deseeded if liked

3 fresh green chillies, finely chopped

1 tsp ground turmeric

3 garlic cloves, crushed

½ tsp pepper

1 tsp paprika

2 tsp white wine vinegar

½ tsp salt

500 g/1 lb 2 oz uncooked peeled king
   prawns (shrimp)

3 tbsp oil

1 onion, chopped very finely

175 ml/6 fl oz/¾ cup water

2 tbsp lemon juice

2 tsp garam masala

sprigs of fresh coriander (cilantro),
   to garnish

COOK'S TIP

Garam masala should be used sparingly and is generally added to foods towards the end of their cooking time. It is also used sprinkled over cooked meats, vegetables and pulses as a garnish.

1 Combine the chillies, spices, vinegar and salt in a non-metallic bowl. Stir in the prawns (shrimp) and leave for 10 minutes.

2 Heat the oil in a large frying pan (skillet) or wok, add the onion and fry for 3–4 minutes until soft.

3 Add the prawns (shrimp) and the contents of the bowl to the pan and stir-fry over a high heat for 2 minutes.

Reduce the heat, add the water and boil for 10 minutes, stirring occasionally, until the water is evaporated and the curry is fragrant.

4 Stir in the lemon juice and garam masala then transfer the mixture to a warm serving dish and garnish with fresh coriander (cilantro) sprigs.

5 Serve garnished with sprigs of fresh coriander (cilantro).

Salmon Yakitori

The Japanese sauce used here combines well with salmon, although it is usually served with chicken.

NUTRITIONAL INFORMATION

Calories 247	Sugars 10g	
Protein 19g	Fat 11g	
Carbohydrate ...12g	Saturates 2g	

 20 MINS   15 MINS

SERVES 4

I N G R E D I E N T S

350 g/12 oz chunky salmon fillet

8 baby leeks

Y A K I T O R I   S A U C E

5 tbsp light soy sauce

5 tbsp fish stock

2 tbsp caster (superfine) sugar

5 tbsp dry white wine

3 tbsp sweet sherry

1 clove garlic, crushed

1 Skin the salmon and cut the flesh into 5 cm/2 inch chunks. Trim the leeks and cut them into 5 cm/2 inch lengths.

2 Thread the salmon and leeks alternately on to 8 pre-soaked wooden skewers. Leave to chill in the refrigerator until required.

3 To make the sauce, place all of the ingredients in a small pan and heat gently, stirring, until the sugar has dissolved.

4 Bring to the boil, then reduce the heat and simmer for 2 minutes. Strain the sauce through a fine sieve (strainer) and leave to cool until it is required.

5 Pour about one-third of the sauce into a small dish and set aside to serve with the kebabs.

6 Brush plenty of the remaining sauce over the skewers and cook directly on the rack.

7 If preferred, place a sheet of oiled kitchen foil on the rack and cook the salmon on that.

8 Barbecue (grill) the salmon and leek kebabs over hot coals for about 10 minutes or until cooked though, turning once.

9 Use a brush to baste frequently during cooking with the remaining sauce in order to prevent the fish and vegetables from drying out. Transfer the kebabs to a large serving platter and serve with a small bowl of the reserved sauce for dipping.

Baked Sea Bass

Sea bass is often paired with subtle oriental flavours. For a special occasion, you may like to bone the fish.

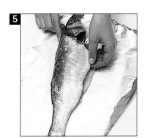

NUTRITIONAL INFORMATION

Calories 140	Sugars 0.1g	
Protein 29g	Fat 1g	
Carbohydrate ...0.1g	Saturates 0.2g	

 10 MINS   15 MINS

SERVES 4–6

I N G R E D I E N T S

2 sea bass, about 1 kg/2 lb 4 oz each, cleaned and scaled

2 spring onions (scallions), green part only, cut into strips

5 cm/2 inch piece ginger, peeled and cut into strips

2 garlic cloves, unpeeled, crushed lightly

2 tbsp mirin or dry sherry

salt and pepper

TO SERVE

pickled sushi ginger (optional)

soy sauce

1 For each fish lay out a double thickness of foil and oil the top piece well, or lay a piece of silicon paper over the foil.

2 Place the fish in the middle and expose the cavity.

3 Divide the spring onion (scallion) and ginger between each cavity. Put a garlic clove in each cavity.

4 Pour over the mirin or dry sherry. Season the fish well.

5 Close the cavities and lay each fish on its side. Bring over the foil and fold the edges together to seal securely. Fold each end neatly.

6 Cook over a medium barbecue (grill) for 15 minutes, turning once.

7 To serve, remove the foil and cut each fish into 2 or 3 pieces.

8 Serve with the pickled ginger (if using) accompanied by soy sauce.

COOK'S TIP

Fresh sea bass is just as delicious when cooked very simply. Stuff the fish with garlic and chopped herbs, brush with olive oil and bake in the oven.

Curried Crab

If you can buy fresh crab, clean the shell and brush lightly with oil and use as a container for the crab meat.

NUTRITIONAL INFORMATION

Calories 272   Sugars 5g
Protein . . . . .27g   Fat 16g
Carbohydrate . . . .5g   Saturates 2g

 5 MINS   15 MINS

SERVES 4

INGREDIENTS

2 tbsp mustard oil

1 tbsp ghee

1 onion, chopped finely

5 cm/2 inch piece ginger root, grated

2 garlic cloves, peeled but left whole

1 tsp ground turmeric

1 tsp salt

1 tsp chilli powder

2 fresh green chillies, chopped

1 tsp paprika

125 g/4½ oz/½ cup brown crab meat

350 g/12 oz/1½ cups white crab meat

250 ml/9 fl oz /1 cup low-fat natural yogurt

1 tsp garam masala

basmati rice, to serve

fresh coriander (cilantro), to garnish

1 Heat the mustard oil in a large, preferably non-stick, frying pan (skillet), wok or saucepan.

2 When it starts to smoke, add the ghee and onion. Stir for 3 minutes over a medium heat until the onion is soft.

3 Stir in the ginger and whole garlic cloves.

4 Add the turmeric, salt, chilli powder, chillies and paprika. Mix thoroughly.

5 Increase the heat and add the crab meat and yogurt. Simmer, stirring occasionally, for 10 minutes until the sauce is thickened slightly.

6 Add garam masala to taste.

7 Serve hot, over plain basmati rice, with the fresh coriander (cilantro) either chopped or in sprigs.

COOK'S TIP

For an unusual combination of flavours, mix the crab meat with segments of grapefruit in a mayonnaise. Sprinkle with slivers of almonds.

Lemony Monkfish Skewers

A simple basting sauce is brushed over these tasty kebabs. When served with crusty bread, they make a perfect light meal.

NUTRITIONAL INFORMATION

Calories 191	Sugars 2g	
Protein 21g	Fat 11g	
Carbohydrate 1g	Saturates 1g	

10 MINS   15 MINS

SERVES 4

INGREDIENTS

450 g/1 lb monkfish tail

2 courgettes (zucchini)

1 lemon

12 cherry tomatoes

8 bay leaves

SAUCE

3 tbsp olive oil

2 tbsp lemon juice

1 tsp chopped, fresh thyme

½ tsp lemon pepper

salt

TO SERVE

green salad leaves

fresh, crusty bread

1 Cut the monkfish into 5 cm/2 inch chunks.

VARIATION

Use plaice (flounder) fillets instead of the monkfish, if you prefer. Allow two fillets per person, and skin and cut each fillet lengthways into two. Roll up each piece and thread them on to the skewers.

2 Cut the courgettes (zucchini) into thick slices and the lemon into wedges.

3 Thread the monkfish, courgettes (zucchini), lemon, tomatoes and bay leaves on to 4 skewers.

4 To make the basting sauce, combine the oil, lemon juice, thyme, lemon pepper and salt to taste in a small bowl.

5 Brush the basting sauce liberally all over the fish, lemon, tomatoes and bay leaves on the skewers.

6 Cook the skewers on the barbecue (grill) for about 15 minutes over medium-hot coals, basting them frequently with the sauce, until the fish is cooked through. Transfer the skewers to plates and serve with green salad leaves and wedges of crusty bread.

Fragrant Tuna Steaks

Fresh tuna steaks are very meaty – they have a firm texture, yet the flesh is succulent. Steaks from the belly are best of all.

NUTRITIONAL INFORMATION

Calories . . . . . . .239 Sugars 0.1g
Protein . . . . .42g Fat 8g
Carbohydrate . . .0.5g Saturates 2g

15 MINS   15 MINS

SERVES 4

INGREDIENTS

4 tuna steaks, 175 g/6 oz each

½ tsp finely grated lime rind

1 garlic clove, crushed

2 tsp olive oil

1 tsp ground cumin

1 tsp ground coriander (cilantro)

pepper

1 tbsp lime juice

fresh coriander (cilantro), to garnish

TO SERVE

avocado relish (see Cook's Tip, below)

lime wedges

tomato wedges

1 Trim the skin from the tuna steaks, rinse and pat dry on absorbent kitchen paper (paper towels).

2 In a small bowl, mix together the lime rind, garlic, olive oil, cumin, ground coriander and pepper to make a paste.

3 Spread the paste thinly on both sides of the tuna. Heat a non-stick, ridged frying pan (skillet) until hot and press the tuna steaks into the pan to seal them. Lower the heat and cook for 5 minutes. Turn the fish over and cook for a further 4–5 minutes until the fish is cooked through. Drain on kitchen paper (paper towels) and transfer to a serving plate.

4 Sprinkle the lime juice and chopped coriander (cilantro) over the fish. Serve with avocado relish (see Cook's Tip), and tomato and lime wedges.

COOK'S TIP

For the avocado relish, peel and chop a small ripe avocado. Mix in 1 tbsp lime juice, 1 tbsp freshly chopped coriander (cilantro), 1 small finely chopped red onion and some chopped fresh mango or tomato. Season to taste.

Char-Grilled Mackerel

The sharpness of the apricot glaze complements the oiliness of the fish and has a delicious hint of ginger.

NUTRITIONAL INFORMATION

Calories 343	Sugars 21g
Protein 23g	Fat 18g
Carbohydrate ...22g	Saturates 4g

 5 MINS   10 MINS

SERVES 4

INGREDIENTS

4 mackerel, about 225 g/8 oz each

400 g/14 oz can apricots in natural juice

3 tbsp dark muscovado sugar

3 tbsp Worcestershire sauce

3 tbsp soy sauce

2 tbsp tomato purée (paste)

1 tsp ground ginger

dash Tabasco sauce

1 clove garlic, crushed (optional)

salt and pepper

1 Clean and gut the mackerel, removing the heads if preferred. Place the fish in a shallow dish.

2 Drain the apricots, reserving the juice. Roughly chop half of the apricots and set aside. Place the remaining apricots in a food processor with the sugar, Worcestershire sauce, soy sauce, tomato purée (paste), ginger, Tabasco sauce and garlic (if using) and process until smooth. Alternatively, chop the apricots and mix with the other ingredients. Season to taste.

3 Pour the sauce over the fish, turning them so that they are well coated on both sides. Leave to chill in the refrigerator until required.

4 Transfer the mackerel to the barbecue (grill) either directly on the rack or on a piece of greased kitchen foil. Barbecue (grill) the mackerel over hot coals for 5–7 minutes, turning once.

5 Spoon any remaining marinade into a saucepan. Add the reserved chopped apricots and about half of the reserved apricot juice and bring to the boil. Reduce the heat and simmer for 2 minutes. Transfer the mackerel to a serving plate and serve with the apricot sauce.

COOK'S TIP

Use a hinged rack if you have one as it will make it much easier to turn the fish during barbecueing (grilling).

Scallop Skewers

As the scallops are marinated, it is not essential that they are fresh; frozen shellfish are fine for a barbecue (grill).

NUTRITIONAL INFORMATION

Calories 182   Sugars 0g
Protein ....29g   Fat 7g
Carbohydrate ....0g   Saturates 1g

30 MINS   10 MINS

SERVES 4

INGREDIENTS

grated zest and juice of 2 limes

2 tbsp finely chopped lemon grass or 1 tbsp lemon juice

2 garlic cloves, crushed

1 green chilli, deseeded and chopped

16 scallops, with corals

2 limes, each cut into 8 segments

2 tbsp sunflower oil

1 tbsp lemon juice

salt and pepper

TO SERVE

60 g/2 oz/1 cup rocket (arugula) salad

200 g/7 oz/3 cups mixed salad leaves (greens)

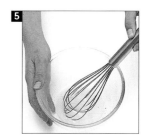

1 Soak 8 skewers in warm water for at least 10 minutes before you use them to prevent the food from sticking.

2 Combine the lime juice and zest, lemon grass, garlic and chilli together in a pestle and mortar or spice grinder to make a paste.

3 Thread 2 scallops on to each of the soaked skewers. Cover the ends with foil to prevent them from burning.

4 Alternate the scallops with the lime segments.

5 Whisk together the oil, lemon juice, salt and pepper to make the dressing.

6 Coat the scallops with the spice paste and place over a medium barbecue (grill), basting occasionally.

7 Cook for 10 minutes, turning once.

8 Toss the rocket (arugula), mixed salad leaves (greens) and dressing together well. Put into a serving bowl.

9 Serve the scallops piping hot, 2 skewers on each plate, with the salad.

Green Fish Curry

This dish has a wonderful fresh, hot, exotic taste resulting from the generous amount of fresh herbs, sharp fresh chillies and coconut milk.

NUTRITIONAL INFORMATION

Calories 223   Sugars 2g

Protein ....44g   Fat 5g

Carbohydrate ....2g   Saturates 1g

5 MINS   20 MINS

SERVES 4

INGREDIENTS

1 tbsp oil

2 spring onions (scallions), sliced

1 tsp cumin seeds, ground

2 fresh green chillies, chopped

1 tsp coriander seeds, ground

4 tbsp chopped fresh coriander (cilantro)

4 tbsp chopped fresh mint

1 tbsp chopped chives

150 ml/¼ pint/⅔ cup coconut milk

4 white fish fillets, about 225 g/8 oz each

salt and pepper

basmati rice, to serve

1 mint sprig, to garnish

1 Heat the oil in a large frying pan (skillet) or shallow saucepan and add the spring onions (scallions).

2 Stir-fry the spring onions (scallions) over a medium heat until they are softened but not coloured.

3 Stir in the cumin, chillies and ground coriander (cilantro), and cook until fragrant.

4 Add the fresh coriander (cilantro), mint, chives and coconut milk and season liberally.

5 Carefully place the fish in the pan and poach for 10–15 minutes until the flesh flakes when tested with a fork.

6 Serve the fish fillets in the sauce with the rice. Garnish with a mint sprig.

COOK'S TIP

Never overcook fish – it is surprising how little time it takes compared to meat. It will continue to cook slightly while keeping warm in the oven and while being dished up and brought to the table.

Plaice with Mushrooms

The moist texture of grilled (broiled) fish is complemented by the texture of the mushrooms.

NUTRITIONAL INFORMATION

Calories 243   Sugars 2g
Protein ....30g   Fat 13g
Carbohydrate ....2g   Saturates 3g

10 MINS   20 MINS

SERVES 4

I N G R E D I E N T S

4 × 150 g/5½ oz white-skinned plaice fillets

2 tbsp lime juice

celery salt and pepper

90 g/3 oz/⅓ cup low-fat spread

300 g/10½ oz/2½ cups mixed small mushrooms such as button, oyster, shiitake, chanterelle or morel, sliced or quartered

4 tomatoes, skinned, seeded and chopped

basil leaves, to garnish

mixed salad, to serve

1 Line a grill (broiler) rack with baking parchment and place the fish on top.

2 Sprinkle over the lime juice and season with celery salt and pepper.

3 Place under a preheated moderate grill (broiler) and cook for 7–8 minutes without turning, until just cooked. Keep warm.

4 Meanwhile, gently melt the low fat spread in a non-stick frying pan (skillet), add the mushrooms and fry for 4–5 minutes over a low heat until cooked through.

5 Gently heat the tomatoes in a small saucepan.

6 Spoon the mushrooms, with any pan juices, and the tomatoes over the plaice.

7 Garnish the grilled (broiled) plaice with the basil leaves and serve with a mixed salad.

COOK'S TIP

Mushrooms are ideal in a low-fat diet, as they are packed full of flavour and contain no fat. More 'meaty' types of mushroom, such as chestnut (crimini), will take slightly longer to cook.

Fish with Black Bean Sauce

Any firm and delicate fish steaks such as salmon or salmon trout can be cooked by the same method.

NUTRITIONAL INFORMATION

Calories 194	Sugars 0.2g	
Protein 27g	Fat 9g	
Carbohydrate 1g	Saturates 1g	

🕑 5 MINS 🕐 20 MINS

SERVES 6

I N G R E D I E N T S

1 sea bass, trout or turbot, weighing about 700g/1 lb 9 oz, cleaned

1 tsp salt

1 tbsp sesame oil

2-3 spring onions (scallions), cut in half lengthways

1 tbsp light soy sauce

1 tbsp Chinese rice wine or dry sherry

1 tbsp finely shredded ginger root

1 tbsp oil

2 tbsp crushed black bean sauce

2 finely shredded spring onions (scallions)

fresh coriander leaves, to garnish (optional)

lemon slices, to garnish

1 Score both sides of the fish with diagonal cuts at 2.5 cm (1 inch) intervals. Rub both the inside and outside of the fish with salt and sesame oil.

2 Place the fish on top of the spring onions (scallions) on a heat-proof platter. Blend the soy sauce and wine with the ginger shreds and pour evenly all over the fish.

3 Place the fish on the platter in a very hot steamer (or inside a wok on a rack), cover and steam vigorously for 12-15 minutes.

4 Heat the oil until hot, then blend in the black bean sauce. Remove the fish from the steamer and place on a serving dish.

5 Pour the hot black bean sauce over the whole length of the fish and place the shredded spring onions (scallions) on top. Place the fish on a platter and serve garnished with coriander leaves (if using) and lemon slices.

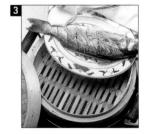

COOK'S TIP

If using fish steaks, rub them with the salt and sesame oil, but do not score with a knife. The fish may require less cooking, depending on the thickness of the steaks – test with a skewer after about 8 minutes to check whether they are done.

Scallops with Mushrooms

Scallops have a rich but delicate flavour. When sautéed with mushrooms and bathed in brandy and cream, they make a really special meal.

NUTRITIONAL INFORMATION

Calories 390	Sugars 1g
Protein 31g	Fat 28g
Carbohydrate 1g	Saturates 4g

5 MINS   10 MINS

SERVES 2

INGREDIENTS

15 g/½ oz/1 tbsp butter

225 g/8 oz shelled queen scallops

1 tbsp olive oil

50 g/1¾ oz oyster mushrooms, sliced

50 g/1¾ oz shiitake mushrooms, sliced

1 garlic clove, chopped

4 spring onions (scallions), white and green parts sliced

3 tbsp double (heavy) cream

1 tbsp brandy

salt and pepper

sprigs of fresh dill, to garnish

basmati rice to serve

1 Heat the butter in a heavy-based frying pan (skillet) and fry the scallops for about 1 minute, turning occasionally.

2 Remove the scallops from the frying pan (skillet) with a perforated spoon and keep warm.

3 Add the olive oil to the pan and heat. Add the mushrooms, garlic and spring onions (scallions) and cook for 2 minutes, stirring constantly.

4 Return the scallops to the pan. Add the double (heavy) cream and brandy, stirring well to mix.

5 Season with salt and pepper to taste and heat to warm through.

6 Garnish with fresh dill sprigs and serve with rice.

COOK'S TIP

Scallops, which consist of a large, round white muscle with bright orange roe, are the most delicious seafood in the prettiest of shells. The rounded half of the shell can be used as a dish in which to serve the scallops.

Baked Trout Mexican-Style

Make this dish as hot or as mild as you like by adjusting the amount of red chilli. The green chillies are milder and add a pungency to the dish.

NUTRITIONAL INFORMATION

Calories 329	Sugars 5g	
Protein 53g	Fat 10g	
Carbohydrate 6g	Saturates 2g	

10 MINS   30 MINS

SERVES 4

INGREDIENTS

4 trout, 225 g/8 oz each

1 small bunch fresh coriander (cilantro)

4 shallots, shredded finely

1 small yellow (bell) pepper, deseeded and
very finely chopped

1 small red (bell) pepper, deseeded and
very finely chopped

2 green chillies, deseeded and
finely chopped

1–2 red chillies, deseeded and
finely chopped

1 tbsp lemon juice

1 tbsp white wine vinegar

2 tsp caster (superfine) sugar

salt and pepper

fresh coriander (cilantro), to garnish

salad leaves, to serve

1 Preheat the oven to 180°C/350°F/Gas Mark 4. Wash the trout and pat dry with kitchen paper (paper towels). Season and stuff with coriander (cilantro) leaves.

2 Place the fish side by side in a shallow ovenproof dish. Sprinkle over the shallots, (bell) peppers and chillies.

3 Mix together the lemon juice, vinegar and sugar in a bowl. Spoon over the trout and season with salt and pepper. Cover the dish and bake for 30 minutes or until the fish is tender and the flesh is opaque.

4 Remove the the fish with a fish slice and drain. Transfer to warm serving plates and spoon the cooking juices over the fish. Garnish with fresh coriander (cilantro) and serve with salad and chilli bean rice (see Cook's Tip).

COOK'S TIP

For the chilli bean rice, cook 225 g/8 oz/1¼ cup long-grain white rice. Drain and rinse a 400 g/14 oz can kidney beans and stir into the rice with 1 tsp each of ground cumin and coriander (cilantro). Stir in 4 tbsp chopped fresh coriander (cilantro) and season.

Oriental Vegetable Noodles

This dish has a mild, nutty flavour from the peanut butter and dry-roasted peanuts.

NUTRITIONAL INFORMATION

Calories 193   Sugars 5g
Protein ....7g   Fat 12g
Carbohydrate ...14g   Saturates 2g

10 MINS   15 MINS

SERVES 4

INGREDIENTS

175 g/6 oz/1½ cups green thread noodles or multi-coloured spaghetti

1 tsp sesame oil

2 tbsp crunchy peanut butter

2 tbsp light soy sauce

1 tbsp white wine vinegar

1 tsp clear honey

125 g/4½ oz daikon (mooli), grated

125 g/4½ oz/1 large carrot, grated

125 g/4½ oz cucumber, shredded finely

1 bunch spring onions (scallions), shredded finely

1 tbsp dry-roasted peanuts, crushed

TO GARNISH

carrot flowers

spring onion (scallion) tassels

1 Bring a large saucepan of water to the boil, add the noodles or spaghetti and cook according to the packet instructions. Drain well and rinse in cold water. Leave in a bowl of cold water until required.

2 To make the peanut butter sauce, put the sesame oil, peanut butter, soy sauce, vinegar, honey and seasoning into a small screw-top jar. Seal and shake well to mix thoroughly.

3 Drain the noodles or spaghetti well, place in a large serving bowl and mix in half the peanut sauce.

4 Using 2 forks, toss in the daikon (mooli), carrot, cucumber and spring onions (scallions). Sprinkle with crushed peanuts and garnish with carrot flowers and spring onion (scallion) tassels. Serve the noodles with the remaining peanut sauce.

COOK'S TIP

There are many varieties of oriental noodles available from oriental markets, delicatessens and supermarkets. Try rice noodles, which contain very little fat and require little cooking; usually soaking in boiling water is sufficient.

Char-Grilled Vegetables

This medley of (bell) peppers, courgettes (zucchini), aubergine (eggplant) and red onion can be served on its own or as an unusual side dish.

NUTRITIONAL INFORMATION

Calories 66   Sugars 7g
Protein . . . . .2g   Fat 3g
Carbohydrate . . . .7g   Saturates 0.5g

15 MINS   15 MINS

SERVES 4

INGREDIENTS

1 large red (bell) pepper

1 large green (bell) pepper

1 large orange (bell) pepper

1 large courgette (zucchini)

4 baby aubergines (eggplant)

2 medium red onions

2 tbsp lemon juice

1 tbsp olive oil

1 garlic clove, crushed

1 tbsp chopped, fresh rosemary or 1 tsp dried rosemary

salt and pepper

TO SERVE

cracked wheat, cooked

tomato and olive relish

1 Halve and deseed the (bell) peppers and cut into even sized pieces, about 2.5 cm/1 inch wide.

2 Trim the courgettes (zucchini), cut in half lengthways and slice into 2.5 cm/1 inch pieces. Place the (bell) peppers and courgettes (zucchini) in a large bowl.

3 Trim the aubergines (eggplant) and quarter them lengthways. Peel both the onions, then cut each one into 8 even-sized wedges.

4 Add the pieces of aubergine (eggplant) and onions to the bowl containing the wedges of (bell) peppers and courgettes (zucchini).

5 In a small bowl, whisk together the lemon juice, olive oil, garlic, rosemary and seasoning.

6 Pour the mixture over the vegetables and stir to coat evenly.

7 Preheat the grill (broiler) to medium. Thread the vegetables on to 8 metal or pre-soaked wooden skewers. Arrange the kebabs on the rack and cook for 10–12 minutes, turning frequently until the vegetables are lightly charred and just softened.

8 Drain the vegetable kebabs and serve on a bed of cracked wheat accompanied with a tomato and olive relish.

Spinach & Orange Salad

This is a refreshing and very nutritious salad. Add the dressing just before serving so that the leaves do not become soggy.

NUTRITIONAL INFORMATION

Calories 126   Sugars 10g
Protein ....3g   Fat 9g
Carbohydrate ...10g   Saturates 1g

 10 MINS   0 MINS

SERVES 4

INGREDIENTS

225 g/8 oz baby spinach leaves

2 large oranges

½ red onion

DRESSING

3 tbsp extra virgin olive oil

2 tbsp freshly squeezed orange juice

2 tsp lemon juice

1 tsp clear honey

½ tsp wholegrain mustard

salt and pepper

1 Wash the spinach leaves under cold running water and then dry them thoroughly on absorbent kitchen paper. Remove any tough stalks and tear the larger leaves into smaller pieces.

2 Slice the top and bottom off each orange with a sharp knife, then remove the peel. Carefully slice between the membranes of the orange to remove the segments. Reserve any juices for the salad dressing.

3 Using a sharp knife, finely chop the onion.

4 Mix together the salad leaves and orange segments and arrange in a serving dish.

5 Scatter the chopped onion over the salad.

6 To make the dressing, whisk together the olive oil, orange juice, lemon juice, honey, mustard and salt and pepper to taste in a small bowl.

7 Pour the dressing over the salad just before serving. Toss the salad well to coat the leaves with the dressing.

VARIATION

Use a mixture of spinach and watercress leaves, if you prefer a slightly more peppery flavour.

Mixed Leaf Salad

Make this green, leafy salad from as many varieties of salad leaves and flowers as you can find to give an unusual effect.

NUTRITIONAL INFORMATION

Calories 51	Sugars 0.1g
Protein 0.1g	Fat 6g
Carbohydrate 1g	Saturates 1g

5 MINS   0 MINS

SERVES 4

INGREDIENTS

½ head frisée (chicory)

½ head feuille de chêne (oak leaf lettuce)
  or quattro stagione

few leaves of radiccio

1 head chicory (endive)

25 g/1 oz/½ cup rocket (arugula) leaves

few sprigs fresh basil or flat-leaf parsley

6 tbsp French dressing

flowers of your choice (see Cook's Tip)

1 Tear the frisée (chicory), feuille de chêne (oak leaf lettuce) and radiccio into manageable pieces.

2 Place the salad leaves (greens) into a large serving bowl, or individual bowls if you prefer.

3 Cut the chicory (endive) into diagonal slices and add to the bowl with the rocket (arugula) leaves, basil or parsley.

4 Pour the dressing over the salad and toss thoroughly. Scatter a mixture of flowers over the top.

COOK'S TIP

Violas, rock geraniums, nasturtiums, chive flowers and pot marigolds add vibrant colours and a sweet flavour to any salad. Use it as a centrepiece at a dinner party, or to liven up a simple everyday meal.

Root Vegetable Salad

This salad of grated vegetables is perfect for a light starter. The peppery flavours of the mooli and radishes are refreshingly pungent.

NUTRITIONAL INFORMATION

Calories 132	Sugars 9g	
Protein 4g	Fat 8g	
Carbohydrate ...12g	Saturates 1g	

 20 MINS   0 MINS

SERVES 4

INGREDIENTS

350 g/12 oz carrots

225 g/8 oz mooli (white radish)

115 g/4 oz radishes

350 g/12 oz celeriac

1 tbsp orange juice

2 sticks celery with leaves, washed and trimmed

100 g/3½ oz assorted salad leaves

25 g/1 oz walnuts, chopped

DRESSING

1 tbsp walnut oil

1 tbsp white wine vinegar

1 tsp wholegrain mustard

½ tsp finely grated orange rind

1 tsp celery seeds

salt and pepper

1 Peel and coarsely grate or very finely shred the carrots, mooli (white radish) and radishes. Set aside in separate bowls.

2 Peel and coarsely grate or finely shred the celeriac and mix with the orange juice.

3 Remove the celery leaves and reserve. Finely chop the celery sticks.

4 Divide the salad leaves among 4 serving plates and arrange the vegetables in small piles on top. Set aside while you make the dressing.

5 Mix all of the dressing ingredients together and season well. Drizzle a little over each salad.

6 Shred the reserved celery leaves and sprinkle over the salad with the chopped walnuts.

COOK'S TIP

Also known as Chinese white radish and daikon, mooli resembles a large white parsnip. It has crisp, slightly pungent flesh, which can be eaten raw or cooked. It is a useful ingredient in stir-fries.

Coleslaw

Home-made coleslaw tastes far superior to any that you can buy. If you make it in advance, add the sunflower seeds just before serving.

NUTRITIONAL INFORMATION

Calories 224	Sugars 8g
Protein 3g	Fat 20g
Carbohydrate 8g	Saturates 3g

10 MINS   5 MINS

SERVES 4

INGREDIENTS

150 ml/5 fl oz/⅔ cup low-fat mayonnaise

150 ml/5 fl oz/⅔ cup low-fat natural yogurt

dash of Tabasco sauce

1 medium head white cabbage

4 carrots

1 green (bell) pepper

2 tbsp sunflower seeds

salt and pepper

1 To make the dressing, combine the mayonnaise, yogurt, Tabasco sauce and salt and pepper to taste in a small bowl. Leave to chill until required.

2 Cut the cabbage in half and then into quarters. Remove and discard the tough centre stalk. Shred the cabbage leaves finely. Wash the leaves and dry them thoroughly.

VARIATION

For a slightly different taste, add one or more of the following ingredients to the coleslaw: raisins, grapes, grated apple, chopped walnuts, cubes of cheese or roasted peanuts.

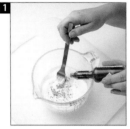  

3 Peel the carrots and shred using a food processor or mandolin. Alternatively, coarsely grate the carrot.

4 Quarter and deseed the (bell) pepper and cut the flesh into thin strips.

5 Combine the vegetables in a large mixing bowl and toss to mix. Pour over the dressing and toss until the vegetables are well coated. Leave to chill in the refrigerator until required.

6 Just before serving, place the sunflower seeds on a baking tray (cookie sheet) and toast them in the oven or under the grill (broiler) until golden brown. Transfer the salad to a large serving dish, scatter with sunflower seeds and serve.

Quick Bean Salad

This attractive-looking salad served with meat from the barbecue (grill) makes a delicious light meal in summer.

NUTRITIONAL INFORMATION

Calories 139   Sugars 5g
Protein . . . . .8g   Fat 3g
Carbohydrate . . .21g   Saturates 0.4g

 10 MINS   0 MINS

SERVES 4

I N G R E D I E N T S

400 g/14 oz can chickpeas (garbanzo beans)

4 carrots

1 bunch spring onions (scallions)

1 medium cucumber

½ tsp salt

½ tsp pepper

3 tbsp lemon juice

1 red (bell) pepper

1 Drain the chickpeas (garbanzo beans) and place in a salad bowl.

2 Using a sharp knife, peel and slice the carrots.

3 Cut the spring onions (scallions) into small pieces.

4 Cut the cucumber into thick quarters.

5 Add the carrots, spring onions (scallions) and cucumber to the chickpeas (garbanzo beans) and mix. Season with the salt and pepper and sprinkle with the lemon juice.

6 Toss the salad ingredients together gently using 2 serving spoons.

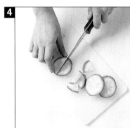

7 Using a sharp knife, slice the red (bell) pepper thinly.

8 Arrange the slices of red (bell) pepper on top of the chickpea (garbanzo bean) salad.

9 Serve the salad immediately or leave to chill in the refrigerator and serve when required.

COOK'S TIP

Using canned chickpeas (garbanzo beans) rather than the dried ones speeds up the cooking time.

Waldorf Chicken Salad

This colourful and healthy dish is a variation of a classic salad. You can use a selection of mixed salad leaves, if preferred.

NUTRITIONAL INFORMATION

Calories	471	Sugars	. . . . .19g
Protein	. . . . .38g	Fat	. . . . .27g
Carbohydrate	. . .20g	Saturates	. . . . . .4g

30 MINS   0 MINS

SERVES 4

INGREDIENTS

500 g/1 lb 2 oz red apples, diced

3 tbsp fresh lemon juice

150 ml/¼ pint/⅔ cup low-fat mayonnaise

1 head of celery

4 shallots, sliced

1 garlic clove, crushed

90 g/3 oz/¾ cup walnuts, chopped

500 g/1 lb 2 oz lean cooked chicken, cubed

1 cos (romaine) lettuce

pepper

sliced apple and walnuts, to garnish

1 Place the apples in a bowl with the lemon juice and 1 tablespoon of mayonnaise. Leave for 40 minutes or until required.

2 Slice the celery very thinly. Add the celery with the shallots, garlic and walnuts to the apple, mix and then add the remaining mayonnaise and blend thoroughly.

3 Add the chicken and mix with the other ingredients.

4 Line a glass salad bowl or serving dish with the lettuce.

5 Pile the chicken salad into the centre, sprinkle with pepper and garnish with apple slices and walnuts.

VARIATION

Instead of the shallots, use spring onions (scallions) for a milder flavour. Trim the spring onions (scallions) and slice finely.

Salad with Garlic Dressing

This is a very quick and refreshing salad using a whole range of colourful ingredients which make it look as good as it tastes.

NUTRITIONAL INFORMATION

Calories ....82 Sugars 5g
Protein ....2g Fat 6g
Carbohydrate ....5g Saturates 1g

10 MINS   0 MINS

SERVES 4

INGREDIENTS

75 g/2¾ oz cucumber, cut into sticks

6 spring onions (scallions), halved

2 tomatoes, seeded and cut into eight

1 yellow (bell) pepper, cut into strips

2 celery sticks, cut into strips

4 radishes, quartered

75 g/2¾ oz rocket

1 tbsp chopped mint, to serve

DRESSING

2 tbsp lemon juice

1 garlic clove, crushed

150 ml/¼ pint/⅔ cup low-fat natural (unsweetened) yogurt

2 tbsp olive oil

salt and pepper

1 To make the salad, mix the cucumber, spring onions (scallions), tomatoes, (bell) pepper, celery, radishes and rocket together in a large serving bowl.

2 To make the dressing, stir the lemon juice, garlic, natural (unsweetened) yogurt and olive oil together.

3 Season well with salt and pepper to taste.

4 Spoon the dressing over the salad and toss to mix. Sprinkle the salad with chopped mint and serve.

COOK'S TIP

Rocket has a distinct warm, peppery flavour which is ideal in green salads. If rocket is unavailable, lamb's lettuce (corn salad) makes a good substitute.

Coronation Salad

This dish is based on Coronation Chicken which was invented to celebrate Queen Victoria's coronation as a symbol of Anglo-Indian links.

NUTRITIONAL INFORMATION

Calories	236	Sugars 24g
Protein	. . . . .7g	Fat 5g
Carbohydrate	. . .43g	Saturates 1g

25 MINS   0 MINS

SERVES 4

INGREDIENTS

1 red (bell) pepper

60 g/2 oz/⅓ cup sultanas (golden raisins)

1 celery stick, sliced

125 g/4½ oz/¾ cup sweetcorn

1 Granny Smith apple, diced

125 g/4½ oz/1 cup white seedless grapes, washed and halved

250 g/9 oz/1½ cups cooked basmati rice

60 g/2 oz/½ cup cooked, peeled prawns (shrimp) (optional)

1 cos (romaine) lettuce, washed and drained

1 tsp paprika to garnish

DRESSING

4 tbsp low-fat mayonnaise

2 tsp mild curry powder

1 tsp lemon juice

1 tsp paprika

pinch of salt

1 Deseed and chop the red (bell) pepper.

2 Combine the sultanas (golden raisins), red (bell) pepper, celery, sweetcorn, apple and grapes in a large bowl. Stir in the rice, and prawns (shrimp), if using.

3 For the dressing, put the mayonnaise, curry powder, lemon juice, paprika and salt into a small bowl and mix well.

4 Pour the dressing over the salad and gently mix until evenly coated.

5 Line the serving plate with cos (romaine) lettuce leaves and spoon on the salad. Sprinkle over the paprika and serve.

COOK'S TIP

Mayonnaise can be bought in varying thicknesses, from the type that you spoon out of the jar to the pouring variety. If you need to thin down mayonnaise for a dressing, simply add water little by little until the desired consistency is reached.

Minted Fennel Salad

This is a very refreshing salad. The subtle liquorice flavour of fennel combines well with the cucumber and mint.

NUTRITIONAL INFORMATION

Calories 90   Sugars 7g
Protein . . . . .4g   Fat 5g
Carbohydrate . . . .7g   Saturates 1g

 25 MINS   0 MINS

SERVES 4

I N G R E D I E N T S

1 bulb fennel

2 small oranges

1 small or ½ large cucumber

1 tbsp chopped mint

1 tbsp virgin olive oil

2 eggs, hard boiled (cooked)

1 Using a sharp knife, trim the outer leaves from the fennel. Slice the fennel bulb thinly into a bowl of water and then sprinkle with lemon juice (see Cook's Tip).

2 Grate the rind of the oranges over a bowl. Using a sharp knife, pare away the orange peel, then segment the orange by carefully slicing between each line of pith. Do this over the bowl in order to retain the juice.

3 Using a sharp knife, cut the cucumber into 12 mm/½ inch rounds and then cut each round into quarters.

4 Add the cucumber to the fennel and orange mixture together with the mint.

5 Pour the olive oil over the fennel and cucumber salad and toss well.

6 Peel and quarter the eggs and use these to decorate the top of the salad. Serve at once.

COOK'S TIP

Fennel will discolour if it is left for any length of time without a dressing. To prevent any discoloration, place it in a bowl of water and sprinkle with lemon juice.

Moroccan Couscous Salad

Couscous is a type of semolina made from durum wheat. It is wonderful in salads as it readily takes up the flavour of the dressing.

NUTRITIONAL INFORMATION

Calories 195	Sugars 15g
Protein 8g	Fat 2g
Carbohydrate ...40g	Saturates 0.3g

15 MINS   15 MINS

SERVES 6

INGREDIENTS

2 cups couscous

1 bunch spring onions (scallions), trimmed and chopped finely

1 small green (bell) pepper, cored, deseeded, and chopped

10 cm/4 inch piece cucumber, chopped

200 g/7 oz can chickpeas (garbanzo beans), rinsed and drained

⅔ cup sultanas (golden raisins)

2 oranges

salt and pepper

lettuce leaves, to serve

sprigs of fresh mint, to garnish

DRESSING

finely grated rind of 1 orange

1 tbsp chopped fresh mint

⅔ cup low-fat natural (unsweetened) yogurt

VARIATION

As an alternative, use bulgar (cracked) wheat instead of the couscous. Rinse thoroughly until the water runs clear, then soak in boiling water for 1 hour. Sieve if necessary.

1 Put the couscous into a bowl and cover with boiling water. Leave it to soak for about 15 minutes to swell the grains, then stir with a fork to separate them.

2 Add the spring onions (scallions), green (bell) pepper, cucumber, chickpeas (garbanzo beans) and sultanas (golden raisins) to the couscous, stirring to combine. Season well with salt and pepper.

3 To make the dressing, mix the orange rind, mint, and yogurt. Pour over the couscous mixture and stir well.

4 Using a sharp serrated knife, remove the peel and pith from the oranges. Cut the flesh into segments, removing all the membrane.

5 Arrange the lettuce leaves on serving plates. Divide the couscous mixture between the plates and arrange the orange segments on top.

6 Garnish with sprigs of fresh mint and serve.

Mussel Salad

A colourful combination of cooked mussels tossed together with char-grilled red (bell) peppers and salad leaves in a lemon dressing.

NUTRITIONAL INFORMATION

Calories ....124 Sugars 5g
Protein ....16g Fat 5g
Carbohydrate ....5g Saturates 1g

40 MINS   10 MINS

SERVES 4

INGREDIENTS

2 large red (bell) peppers

350 g/12 oz cooked shelled mussels, thawed if frozen

1 head of radicchio

25 g/1 oz rocket (arugula) leaves

8 cooked New Zealand mussels in their shells

TO SERVE

lemon wedges

crusty bread

DRESSING

1 tbsp olive oil

1 tbsp lemon juice

1 tsp finely grated lemon rind

2 tsp clear honey

1 tsp French mustard

1 tbsp snipped fresh chives

salt and pepper

1 Preheat the grill (broiler) to hot. Halve and deseed the (bell) peppers and place them skin-side up on the rack.

2 Cook for 8–10 minutes until the skin is charred and blistered and the flesh is soft. Leave to cool for 10 minutes, then peel off the skin.

3 Slice the (bell) pepper flesh into thin strips and place in a bowl. Gently mix in the shelled mussels and set aside until required.

4 To make the dressing, mix all of the ingredients until well blended.

5 Mix into the (bell) pepper and mussel mixture until coated.

6 Remove the central core of the radicchio and shred the leaves. Place in a serving bowl with the rocket (arugula) leaves and toss together.

7 Pile the mussel mixture into the centre of the leaves and arrange the large mussels in their shells around the edge of the dish. Serve with lemon wedges and crusty bread.

Sweet & Sour Fruit

This mixture of fresh and canned fruit, which has a sweet and sour flavour, is very cooling, especially in the summer.

NUTRITIONAL INFORMATION

Calories	240	Sugars	........58g
Protein	.........2g	Fat	..........0.4g
Carbohydrate	...60g	Saturates	......0g

 5 MINS   0 MINS

SERVES 4

INGREDIENTS

400 g/14 oz can mixed fruit cocktail

400 g/14 oz can guavas

2 large bananas

3 apples (optional)

1 tsp ground black pepper

1 tsp salt

½ tsp ground ginger

2 tbsp lemon juice

fresh mint leaves, to garnish

1 Drain the can of mixed fruit cocktail and place the fruit in a deep mixing bowl.

2 Mix the the drained fruit cocktail wth the guavas and their syrup so that the fruit is well coated.

3 Peel the bananas and cut into thick slices.

4 Peel the apples (optional) and cut into dice.

5 Add the fresh fruit to the bowl containing the canned fruit and mix together.

6 Add the ground black pepper, salt and ginger and stir to mix. Add the lemon juice to prevent the banana and apple from turning brown and mix again.

7 Serve the sweet and sour fruit as a snack garnished with a few fresh mint leaves.

COOK'S TIP

Guavas are tropical fruits with a powerful, exotic smell. You may find fresh guavas in specialist shops and large supermarkets, but the canned variety is more widely available. Surprisingly, they have a higher vitamin C content than many citrus fruits.

Carrot & Orange Salad

A crunchy and colourful, sweet and savoury dish which would also make an excellent appetizer.

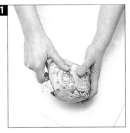

NUTRITIONAL INFORMATION

Calories ....194 Sugars 25g
Protein ....6g Fat 8g
Carbohydrate ...26g Saturates 1g

 20 MINS   0 MINS

SERVES 4

I N G R E D I E N T S

500 g/1 lb 2 oz celeriac (celery root)

2 tbsp orange juice

350 g/12 oz/4 carrots, sliced finely

2 celery sticks, chopped finely

25 g/1 oz/1 cup celery leaves

4 oranges

25 g/1 oz/¼ cup walnut pieces

D R E S S I N G

1 tbsp walnut oil

½ tsp grated orange rind

3 tbsp orange juice

1 tbsp white wine vinegar

1 tsp clear honey

salt and pepper

1 Trim and peel the celeriac (celery root) and slice or grate finely into a bowl. Add the orange juice and toss together.

2 Mix in the carrots, celery and celery leaves. Cover and chill while preparing the oranges.

3 Slice off the tops and bottoms from the oranges. Using a sharp knife, slice off the skin, taking the pith away at the same time. Cut out the orange flesh by slicing along the side of the membranes dividing the segments. Gently mix the segments into the celeriac (celery root) mixture.

4 To make the dressing, place all the ingredients in a small screw-top jar. Seal and shake well to mix.

5 Pile the vegetable mixture on to a plate. Sprinkle over the walnut pieces and serve with the dressing.

COOK'S TIP

Celeriac (celery root) is a variety of celery with a bulbous, knobbly root. It has a rough, light brown skin and creamy white flesh and is delicious raw or cooked.

Tomato Salsa

This salad is used extensively in Mexican cooking and served as a dip or a relish, and is eaten as an accompaniment to almost any dish.

NUTRITIONAL INFORMATION

Calories 10   Sugars 2g
Protein . . . . .0.4g   Fat 0.1g
Carbohydrate . . . .2g   Saturates 0g

10 MINS   0 MINS

SERVES 4

INGREDIENTS

4 ripe red tomatoes

1 medium red onion or 6 spring onions (scallions)

1–2 garlic cloves, crushed (optional)

2 tbsp chopped fresh coriander (cilantro)

½ red or green chilli (optional)

finely grated rind of ½–1 lemon or lime

1–2 tbsp lemon or lime juice

pepper

1 Chop the tomatoes fairly finely and evenly, and put into a bowl. They must be firm and a good strong red colour for the best results, but if preferred, they may be peeled by placing them in boiling water for about 20 seconds and then plunging into cold water. The skins should then slip off easily when they are nicked with a knife.

2 Peel and slice the red onion thinly, or trim the spring onions (scallions) and cut into thin slanting slices; add to the tomatoes with the garlic and coriander (cilantro) and mix lightly.

3 Remove the seeds from the red or green chilli (if using) chop the flesh very finely and add to the salad. Treat the chillies with care; do not touch your eyes or face after handling them until you have washed your hands thoroughly. Chilli juices can burn.

4 Add the lemon or lime rind and juice to the salsa, and mix well. Transfer to a serving bowl and sprinkle with pepper.

COOK'S TIP

If you don't like the distinctive flavour of fresh coriander (cilantro), you can replace it with flat-leaf parsley instead.

Aubergine (Eggplant) Curry

This is a rich vegetable dish, ideal served with a tandoori chicken and naan bread. It is also delicious served as a vegetarian dish with rice.

NUTRITIONAL INFORMATION

Calories 73   Sugars 6g
Protein ....3g   Fat 4g
Carbohydrate ....6g   Saturates 1g

15 MINS   15 MINS

SERVES 6

INGREDIENTS

2 whole aubergines (eggplants)

225 ml/8 fl oz/1 cup low-fat natural (unsweetened) yogurt

2 cardamom pods

½ tsp ground turmeric

1 dried red chilli

½ tsp coriander seeds

½ tsp ground black pepper

1 tsp garam masala

1 clove

2 tbsp sunflower oil

1 onion, sliced lengthways

2 garlic cloves, crushed

1 tbsp grated ginger root

6 ripe tomatoes, peeled, deseeded and quartered

fresh coriander (cilantro), to garnish

1 If you have a gas cooker, roast the 2 aubergines (eggplants) over a naked flame, turning frequently, until charred and black all over This should take about 5 minutes. Peel under running cold water. Cut off the stem end and discard.

2 Put the peeled aubergines (eggplants) into a large bowl and mash lightly with a fork. Stir in the yogurt.

3 Grind together the cardamom pods, turmeric, red chilli, coriander seeds, black pepper, garam masala and clove in a large pestle and mortar or spice grinder.

4 Heat the oil in a wok or heavy frying pan (skillet) over a moderate heat and cook the onion, garlic and ginger root until soft. Add the tomatoes and ground spices, and stir well.

5 Add the aubergine (eggplant) mixture to the pan and stir well. Cook for 5 minutes over a gentle heat, stirring constantly, until all the flavours are combined, and some of the liquid has evaporated.

6 Serve the aubergine (eggplant) immediately, garnished with coriander (cilantro).

Raitas

Raitas are very easy to prepare, very versatile and have a cooling effect which will be appreciated if you are serving hot, spicy dishes.

NUTRITIONAL INFORMATION

Calories	.33	Sugars	.5g
Protein	.3g	Fat	.0.4g
Carbohydrate	.5g	Saturates	.0.3g

 10 MINS   5 MINS

SERVES 4

INGREDIENTS

MINT RAITA

200 ml/7 fl oz/¾ cup low-fat natural (unsweetened) yogurt

50 ml/2 fl oz/4 tbsp water

1 small onion, finely chopped

½ tsp mint sauce

½ tsp salt

3 fresh mint leaves, to garnish

CUCUMBER RAITA

225 g/8 oz cucumber

1 medium onion

½ tsp salt

½ tsp mint sauce

300 ml/10 fl oz/1¼ cups low-fat natural (unsweetened) yogurt

150 ml/¼ pint/⅔ cup water

fresh mint leaves, to garnish

AUBERGINE (EGGPLANT) RAITA

1 medium aubergine (eggplant)

1 tsp salt

1 small onion, finely chopped

2 green chillies, finely chopped

200 ml/7 fl oz/¾ cup low-fat natural (unsweetened) yogurt

3 tbsp water

 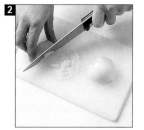 

1 To make the mint raita, place the yogurt in a bowl and whisk with a fork. Gradually whisk in the water. Add the onion, mint sauce and salt and blend together. Garnish with mint leaves.

2 To make the cucumber raita, peel and slice the cucumber. Chop the onion finely. Place the cucumber and onion in a large bowl, then add the salt and the mint sauce. Add the yogurt and the water and

place the mixture in a liquidizer and blend well. Serve garnished with mint leaves.

3 To make the aubergine (eggplant) raita, remove the top end of the aubergine (eggplant) and chop the rest into small pieces. Boil in a pan of water until soft, then drain and mash. Add the salt, onion and green chillies, mixing well. Whip the yogurt with the water and add to the mixture and mix thoroughly.

Spicy Cauliflower

This is a perfectly delicious way to serve cauliflower. It can be enjoyed as a salad or at a picnic, or as a side dish to a main meal.

NUTRITIONAL INFORMATION

Calories	68	Sugars	. . . . .3g
Protein	. . . . .5g	Fat	. . . . .4g
Carbohydrate	. . . .4g	Saturates	. . . . . .1g

5 MINS   15 MINS

SERVES 4

INGREDIENTS

500 g/1 lb 2 oz cauliflower, cut into florets

1 tbsp sunflower oil

1 garlic clove

½ tsp turmeric

1 tsp cumin seeds, ground

1 tsp coriander seeds, ground

1 tsp yellow mustard seeds

12 spring onions (scallions), sliced finely

salt and pepper

1 Blanch the cauliflower in boiling water, drain and set aside. Cauliflower holds a lot of water, which tends to make it over-soft, so turn the florets upside-down at this stage and you will end up with a crisper result.

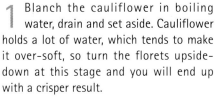

COOK'S TIP

For a special occasion this dish looks great made with baby cauliflowers instead of florets. Peel off most of the outer leaves, leaving a few for decoration, and blanch the baby cauliflowers whole for 4 minutes and drain. Continue as in step 2.

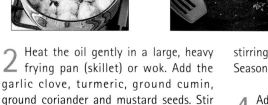

2 Heat the oil gently in a large, heavy frying pan (skillet) or wok. Add the garlic clove, turmeric, ground cumin, ground coriander and mustard seeds. Stir well and cover the pan.

3 When you hear the mustard seeds popping, add the spring onions (scallions) and stir. Cook for 2 minutes, stirring constantly, to soften them a little. Season to taste.

4 Add the cauliflower and stir for 3–4 minutes until coated completely with the spices and thoroughly heated.

5 Remove the garlic clove and serve immediately.

Sesame Seed Chutney

This chutney is delicious served with spiced rice dishes, and also makes an unusual filling to spread in sandwiches.

NUTRITIONAL INFORMATION

Calories	120	Sugars	.........0g
Protein	.........4g	Fat	..........12g
Carbohydrate	...0.2g	Saturates	......2g

 10 MINS   5 MINS

SERVES 4

INGREDIENTS

8 tbsp sesame seeds

2 tbsp water

½ bunch fresh coriander (cilantro)

3 fresh green chillies, chopped

1 tsp salt

2 tsp lemon juice

chopped red chilli, to garnish

1 Place the sesame seeds in a large, heavy-based saucepan and dry roast them. Set the sesame seeds aside to cool.

2 Once cooled, place the sesame seeds in a food processor or pestle and mortar and grind well to form a fine powder.

3 Add the water to the sesame seeds and mix thoroughly to form a smooth paste.

4 Using a sharp knife, finely chop the coriander (cilantro).

5 Add the chillies and coriander (cilantro) to the sesame seed paste and grind once again.

6 Add the salt and lemon juice to the mixture and grind once again.

7 Remove the mixture from the food processor or pestle and mortar and transfer to a serving dish. Garnish with red chilli and serve.

COOK'S TIP

Dry roasting brings out the flavour of dried spices and takes just a few minutes. You will be able to tell when the spices are ready because of the wonderful fragrance that develops. Stir the spices constantly to ensure that they do not burn.

Colcannon

This is an old Irish recipe, usually served with a piece of bacon, but it is equally delicious with chicken or fish.

NUTRITIONAL INFORMATION

Calories . . . . .102 Sugars 4g
Protein . . . . .4g Fat 4g
Carbohydrate . . .14g Saturates 2g

5 MINS   35 MINS

SERVES 4

INGREDIENTS

225 g/8 oz green cabbage, shredded

85 ml/3 fl oz/⅓ cup skimmed milk

225 g/8 oz floury (mealy) potatoes, diced

1 large leek, chopped

pinch of grated nutmeg

15 g/½ oz/1 tbsp butter, melted

salt and pepper

1 Bring a large saucepan of salted water to the boil, add the shredded cabbage and cook for 7–10 minutes. Drain thoroughly and set aside.

2 Meanwhile, in a separate saucepan, bring the milk to the boil and add the potatoes and leek. Reduce the heat and simmer for 15–20 minutes or until they are cooked through.

COOK'S TIP

There are many different varieties of cabbage, which produce hearts at varying times of year, so you can be sure of being able to make this delicious cabbage dish all year round.

3 Stir in the grated nutmeg and mash the potatoes and leeks together.

4 Add the drained cabbage to the potatoes and mix well.

5 Spoon the potato and cabbage mixture into a serving dish, making a hollow in the centre with the back of a spoon.

6 Pour the melted butter into the hollow and serve the colcannon immediately.

Thai Fragrant Coconut Rice

Basmati rice is cooked with creamed coconut, lemon grass, fresh ginger and spices to make a wonderfully aromatic, fluffy rice.

NUTRITIONAL INFORMATION

Calories	258	Sugars	.......0.4g
Protein	.........5g	Fat	...........6g
Carbohydrate	...51g	Saturates	......4g

 5 MINS   20 MINS

SERVES 4–6

INGREDIENTS

2.5 cm/1 inch piece ginger root, peeled and sliced

2 cloves

1 piece lemon grass, bruised and halved

2 tsp ground nutmeg

1 cinnamon stick

1 bay leaf

2 small thin strips lime zest

1 tsp salt

25 g/1 oz creamed coconut, chopped

600 ml/1 pint/2½ cups water

350 g/12 oz/1¾ cups basmati rice

ground pepper

1 Place the ginger, cloves, lemon grass, nutmeg, cinnamon stick, bay leaf, lime zest, salt, creamed coconut and water in a large, heavy-based pan and bring slowly to the boil.

2 Add the rice, stir well, then cover and simmer, over a very gentle heat, for about 15 minutes or until all the liquid has been absorbed and the rice is tender but still has a bite to it.

3 Alternatively, bring the rice to the boil then cover tightly and turn off the heat. Leave for 20–25 minutes before removing the lid – the rice will be perfectly cooked.

4 Remove from the heat, add pepper to taste, then fluff up the rice with a fork.

5 Remove the large pieces of spices before serving.

COOK'S TIP

When using a whole stem of lemon grass (rather than chopped lemon grass), beat it well to bruise it so that the flavour is fully released. Lemon zest or a pared piece of lemon peel can be used instead.

Mixed Fruit Brûlées

Traditionally a rich mixture made with cream, this fruit-based version is just as tempting using natural (unsweetened) yogurt as a topping.

NUTRITIONAL INFORMATION

Calories ....165 Sugars 21g
Protein ....5g Fat 7g
Carbohydrate ...21g Saturates 5g

🍴 5 MINS   🕐 5 MINS

SERVES 4

INGREDIENTS

450 g/1 lb prepared assorted summer fruits (such as strawberries, raspberries, blackcurrants, redcurrants and cherries), thawed if frozen

150 ml/5 fl oz/¾ cup half-fat double (heavy) cream alternative

150 ml/5 fl oz/¾ cup low-fat natural fromage frais (unsweetened yogurt)

1 tsp vanilla essence (extract)

4 tbsp demerara (brown crystal) sugar

1 Divide the prepared strawberries, raspberries, blackcurrants, redcurrants and cherries evenly among 4 small heatproof ramekin dishes.

2 Mix together the half-fat cream alternative, fromage frais (unsweetened yogurt) and vanilla essence (extract) until well combined.

3 Generously spoon the mixture over the fruit in the ramekin dishes, to cover the fruit completely.

4 Preheat the grill (broiler) to hot.

5 Top each serving with 1 tbsp demerara (brown crystal) sugar and grill (broil) the desserts for 2–3 minutes, until the sugar melts and begins to caramelize. Leave to stand for a couple of minutes before serving.

COOK'S TIP

Look out for half-fat creams, in single and double (light and heavy) varieties. They are good substitutes for occasional use. Alternatively, in this recipe, omit the cream and double the quantity of fromage frais (yogurt) for a lower fat version.

Chocolate & Pineapple Cake

Decorated with thick yogurt and canned pineapple, this is a low-fat cake, but it is by no means lacking in flavour.

NUTRITIONAL INFORMATION

Calories 199   Sugars 19g
Protein . . . . .5g   Fat 9g
Carbohydrate . . .28g   Saturates 3g

10 MINS   25 MINS

SERVES 9

I N G R E D I E N T S

150 g/5½ oz/⅔ cup low-fat spread

125 g/4½ oz caster (superfine) sugar

100 g/3½ oz/¾ cup self-raising flour, sieved (strained)

3 tbsp cocoa powder, sieved (strained)

1½ tsp baking powder

2 eggs

225g/8 oz can pineapple pieces in natural juice

125 ml/4 fl oz/½ cup low-fat thick natural yogurt

about 1 tbsp icing (confectioners') sugar

grated chocolate, to decorate

1 Lightly grease a 20 cm/8 inch square cake tin (pan).

2 Place the low-fat spread, caster (superfine) sugar, flour, cocoa powder, baking powder and eggs in a large mixing bowl. Beat with a wooden spoon or electric hand whisk until smooth.

3 Pour the cake mixture into the prepared tin (pan) and level the surface. Bake in a preheated oven, 190°C/325°F/Gas Mark 5, for 20-25 minutes or until springy to the touch. Leave to cool slightly in the tin (pan)

before transferring to a wire rack to cool completely.

4 Drain the pineapple, chop the pineapple pieces and drain again. Reserve a little pineapple for decoration, then stir the rest into the yogurt and sweeten to taste with icing (confectioners') sugar.

5 Spread the pineapple and yogurt mixture over the cake and decorate with the reserved pineapple pieces. Sprinkle with the grated chocolate.

Tropical Fruit Fool

Fruit fools are always popular, and this light, tangy version will be no exception. Use your favourite fruits in this recipe if you prefer.

NUTRITIONAL INFORMATION

Calories 149   Sugars 25g
Protein . . . . .6g   Fat 0.4g
Carbohydrate . . .32g   Saturates 0.2g

35 MINS   0 MINS

SERVES 4

INGREDIENTS

1 medium ripe mango

2 kiwi fruit

1 medium banana

2 tbsp lime juice

½ tsp finely grated lime rind, plus extra to decorate

2 medium egg whites

425 g/15 oz can low-fat custard

½ tsp vanilla essence (extract)

2 passion fruit

1 To peel the mango, slice either side of the smooth, flat central stone. Roughly chop the flesh and blend the fruit in a food processor or blender until smooth. Alternatively, mash with a fork.

VARIATION

Other tropical fruits to try include paw-paw (papaya) purée, with chopped pineapple and dates or pomegranate seeds to decorate. Or make a summer fruit fool by using strawberry purée, topped with raspberries and blackberries and cherries.

2 Peel the kiwi fruit, chop the flesh into small pieces and place in a bowl. Peel and chop the banana and add to the bowl. Toss all of the fruit in the lime juice and rind and mix well.

3 In a grease-free bowl, whisk the egg whites until stiff and then gently fold in the custard and vanilla essence (extract) until thoroughly mixed.

4 In 4 tall glasses, alternately layer the chopped fruit, mango purée and custard mixture, finishing with the custard on top. Leave to chill in the refrigerator for 20 minutes.

5 Halve the passion fruits, scoop out the seeds and spoon the passion fruit over the fruit fools. Decorate each serving with the extra lime rind and serve.

NOTE

This book uses metric and imperial measurements. Follow the same units of
measurement throughout; do not mix metric and imperial. All spoon measurements
are level: teaspoons are assumed to be 5 ml and tablespoons are assumed to be 15 ml.
Unless otherwise stated, milk is assumed to be full fat, eggs and individual vegetables
such as potatoes are medium and pepper is freshly ground black pepper.

The nutritional information provided for each recipe is per serving or per person.
Optional ingredients, variations or serving suggestions have not been included in the
calculations. The times given for each recipe are an approximate guide only because
the preparation times may differ according to the techniques used by different
people and the cooking times may vary as a result of the type of oven used.

Recipes using raw or very lightly cooked eggs should be
avoided by infants, the elderly, pregnant women, convalescents
and anyone suffering from an illness.

ROSES, ROSES, RIOTING

Set off by rose-pink walls and touches of polished mahogany, our English Rose motifs create a rustic bower on everything they touch, unifying a set of disparate pieces of furniture from many periods. The curvaceous pine bedstead and washstand get the most elaborate treatment, in vivid colours picked up by bands of bright rosy pink against an ivory background. You could easily use this approach to lend a new lease of life to a set of pine furniture that is beginning to look dreary. As a base colour, use ivory matt emulsion over acrylic primer, smoothed over with fine sandpaper, or vary the effect by introducing another pale shade on some of the pieces, like the bedside cupboard and

EVERYWHERE

charming plant stand, which are base-coated in the palest of greens. Note that transparent watercolour paints can only be used over pale backgrounds. Anything darker will show through the decoration, altering the effect unless you are prepared to undertake a complex 'whiting out' process first. The tall screen, made up simply of panels of

medium-density-fibreboard, gets the most watery, painterly treatment: rose clusters clambering up the panels and centring the cut-out tops. With such a strong thematic link between the painted pieces, the remaining items can be of the simplest origins, like the Lloyd Loom chair shown here, some pale dhurry rugs, or a faded quilt.

PAINTING WITH A PATTERN

With our patterns to guide you, and photographs to inspire you, professional-looking decoration is a breeze, even for beginners.

• Shown here are the steps involved in tracing off and colouring in the pretty border design shown on the washstand where it 'frames' more complex floral motifs. In two softly contrasting 'rosy' colours, pink and green, this simple design gives useful practice in handling the watercolour medium.

• Throughout we used artists' gouache tube colours, a convenient watercolour medium favoured by professionals, and mixed them with gum arabic, a clear medium sold by artists' suppliers, varying the amount of gum arabic according to the transparency or vividness required.

• Gum arabic makes the paint easier to control, giving smoothness to your brushwork.

• Use soft watercolour brushes, in sizes from fine to medium. There is no need to buy expensive sable brushes – synthetic bristles or mixed hair are fine.

Note: Transparent watercolour paint is inherently more fragile than emulsion and needs 'fixing' on completion of decoration, before you proceed to further varnishing, antiquing etc. All the decoration in this series was fixed with a rapid blast of spray varnish, available from artists' suppliers.

MATERIALS CHECKLIST

WELL-SHARPENED HARD LEAD PENCIL, SCISSORS, MASKING TAPE, OLD PLATE FOR USE AS A PALETTE, WATER JAR, KITCHEN PAPER OR TISSUES, RULER OR TAPE FOR POSITIONING MOTIFS, SPRAY VARNISH.

TUBES OF GOUACHE PAINT IN ALIZARIN ROSE MADDER, PERMANENT GREEN DEEP, FLAKE WHITE, ULTRAMARINE, RAW SIENNA AND YELLOW OCHRE.

SMALL BOTTLE OF GUM ARABIC FOR DILUTING GOUACHE COLOUR.

WATERCOLOUR BRUSHES FROM MEDIUM TO FINE.

COLOUR RECIPES

(A) PERMANENT GREEN DEEP, ULTRAMARINE AND FLAKE WHITE

(B) ALIZARIN ROSE MADDER PLUS FLAKE WHITE

(C) ULTRAMARINE PLUS PERMANENT GREEN DEEP

(D) COLOUR B PLUS A TOUCH OF RAW SIENNA

1 THE BORDER MOTIF OF INTERTWINED RIBBONS IS TRACED DOWN WITH A SHARP PENCIL THROUGH THE TRANSFER PAPER. CUTTING BOTH THE TRACING AND TRANSFER PAPER TO SIZE SPEEDS UP THE WORK.

2 THIS SHOWS HOW ONE COMPLETED SECTION IS MARRIED UP TO THE NEXT BEFORE CONTINUING THE TRACING PROCESS.

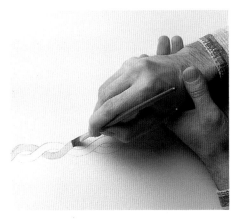

3 USING COLOUR A AND A FLAT BRUSH, THE PALE GREEN RIBBON IS FILLED IN. NOTE HOW THE SPARE HAND IS BEING USED TO SUPPORT AND GUIDE THE PAINTING HAND.

4 WITH COLOUR B, AND THE SAME BRUSH RINSED AND DRIED, THE SECOND RIBBON IS ADDED, SECTION BY SECTION.

5 A PAINTERLY TOUCH WHICH BRINGS THE BORDER TO LIFE: USING THE SAME BRUSH BUT A STRONGER SHADE OF GREEN (MORE GOUACHE, LESS GUM ARABIC) DEEPEN THE GREEN AS SHOWN, USING A PECKY MOTION TO GIVE A RUN OF LITTLE CROSS-HATCHED LINES RATHER THAN A FLUID STROKE.

6 THE SAME PROCESS HAS BEEN REPEATED IN COLOUR B FOR THE PINK RIBBON. THIS USE OF THE BRUSH GIVES A SUGGESTION OF CRISP FABRIC SUCH AS RIBBON RATHER THAN MERE ROUNDED 'WORMS' OF COLOUR.

1 FILL IN THE SMALLEST OF THE THREE SCROLL SHAPES THAT MAKE UP THIS STYLIZED ROPE BORDER USING COLOUR A AND A MEDIUM-SIZED WATERCOLOUR BRUSH.

2 COLOUR C AND A FINER BRUSH ARE USED TO PLACE THE SLENDER CALLIGRAPHIC FLOURISHES UNDER THE PREVIOUS SHAPES.

3 USING COLOUR D AND THE SAME BRUSH, RINSED AND DRIED, A TWIN OF THE PREVIOUSLY COMPLETED SHAPE IS BRUSHED ALONGSIDE. ULTRA-SIMPLE DESIGNS LIKE THIS NEED PRECISE EXECUTION, SO PRACTISE THE BRUSHWORK TILL YOU FEEL EASY WITH IT.

Having learnt how to handle and enjoy this attractive medium, and how to use the tonal range it offers, you are now ready to tackle a more ambitious project like our decorated screen. If possible paint each panel separately, laying it flat on a table or propping it at an angle if you find this easier.

1 THIS SHOWS THE TRACED-DOWN FLORAL MOTIF BEING FILLED IN WITH COLOUR E USING A MEDIUM-FINE WATERCOLOUR BRUSH. AFTER FILLING IN THE LEAVES WITH THE PALER SHADE, WORK A LITTLE MORE GOUACHE INTO THE MIXTURE FOR EMPHASIS.

2 MORE LEAVES AND A FEW STALKS HAVE NOW BEEN ADDED TO BUILD UP THE MOTIF. NOTE THE EFFECT YOU SHOULD BE AIMING FOR: FINE, DARK ACCENTS ON A PREVAILINGLY WATERY BASE COLOUR.

3 COLOUR F IS USED BOTH TO PAINT IN THE THICKER STEMS AND TO SOFTEN AND WARM THE LEAVES HERE AND THERE.

7 THE ROSES AT LAST, USING QUITE DIFFERENT COLOURS, AND A CLEVER TECHNIQUE BORROWED FROM SCANDINAVIAN FOLK 'ROSEMALING' PAINTERS. A ROUND BRUSH AND A FLAT BRUSH ARE NEEDED.

8 PRACTISE MAKING PETAL SHAPES WITH THE ROUND BRUSH ON THE MIXING PLATE, USING THE FLAKE WHITE TINGED EVER SO SLIGHTLY WITH ALIZARIN ROSE MADDER.

9 USING THE PETAL TECHNIQUE YOU PRACTISED ON THE PLATE, NOW ADD THE CRISP PINK FRILL EDGING TO THE PETALS FILLED IN WITH WHITE.

4 USE COLOUR F AND A FINE BRUSH TO WASH IN SOME LIVELY VEINING ON THE LEAVES, TO CRISP UP THE STEMS, AND TO ADD A TOUCH OF EXPRESSIVENESS TO THE DESIGN.

5 A LITTLE FLAKE WHITE ADDED TO COLOUR F IS USED TO SOFTEN AND HIGHLIGHT THE LEAF SHAPES HERE AND THERE.

6 COLOUR G STRIKES A WARM NOTE ALONG THE ROSE STEMS FOR A TOUCH OF REALISM WHICH 'LIFTS' THE WHOLE DESIGN.

10 THE SECOND ROSE IS NOW ALMOST COMPLETE, PAINTED USING EXACTLY THE SAME TECHNIQUE.

11 THE GOLDEN HEARTS ARE BRUSHED IN WITH COLOUR H, AND THEN BROUGHT TO LIFE WITH TINY DOTS OF COLOUR J DROPPED IN WITH THE POINT OF A FINE BRUSH.

12 THE SAME COLOURS ARE USED TO FILL IN BUDS AND HALF-OPENED BLOOMS, AGAIN MAKING USE OF THE FLAT BRUSH TECHNIQUE TO SHADE THE PETALS DELICATELY.

COLOUR RECIPES

(E) PERMANENT GREEN DEEP PLUS ULTRAMARINE AND A LITTLE FLAKE WHITE

(F) RAW SIENNA AND A TRACE OF COLOUR E

(G) RAW SIENNA PLUS ALIZARIN ROSE MADDER

(H) YELLOW OCHRE PLUS FLAKE WHITE

(J) RAW SIENNA

A bit more creative leeway comes in arranging various of the pattern elements to form the clambering border of leaves and flowers which runs up both sides of each screen panel. Use the same colours, in the same graded tones, as for the central cluster on the preceding page.

1 THIS SHOWS HOW THE BORDER IS BUILT UP BY CUTTING AROUND SEPARATE PATTERN ELEMENTS AND TRYING OUT VARIOUS ARRANGEMENTS THAT LOOK NATURAL.

2 HAVING FIXED ON A 'MOVEMENT' TO FOLLOW, THE ELEMENTS OF THE BORDER PATTERN ARE TRACED DOWN THROUGH THE BLUE TRANSFER PAPER ON TO THE PIECE OF FURNITURE.

3 AS BEFORE, THE LEAF SPRAYS ARE WASHED IN USING COLOUR E, BEFORE ADDING FINE EMPHASIS WITH COLOUR F. WITHOUT BEING SLAVISHLY NATURALISTIC, A VARIETY OF SUBTLE COLOUR IS AIMED AT.

4 THE DEFINING PROCESS CONTINUES SLOWLY ACROSS THE WHOLE MOTIF, CREATING A BALANCED UNIVERSALITY OF TONE. TRY TO AVOID MONOTONOUS PERFECTION – MAKE SOME LEAVES MORE EMPHATIC, OTHERS MORE YELLOWY AND MISTY LOOKING.

5 USING A FINE BRUSH, NOW WORK IN THE STEMS AND STALKS TO GIVE THE MOTIF STRUCTURE, USING COLOUR F.

THE INSTRUCTIONS FOR PAINTING THIS BORDER ARE CONTINUED ON THE PAGE FOLLOWING YOUR TRACE-DOWN PATTERNS.

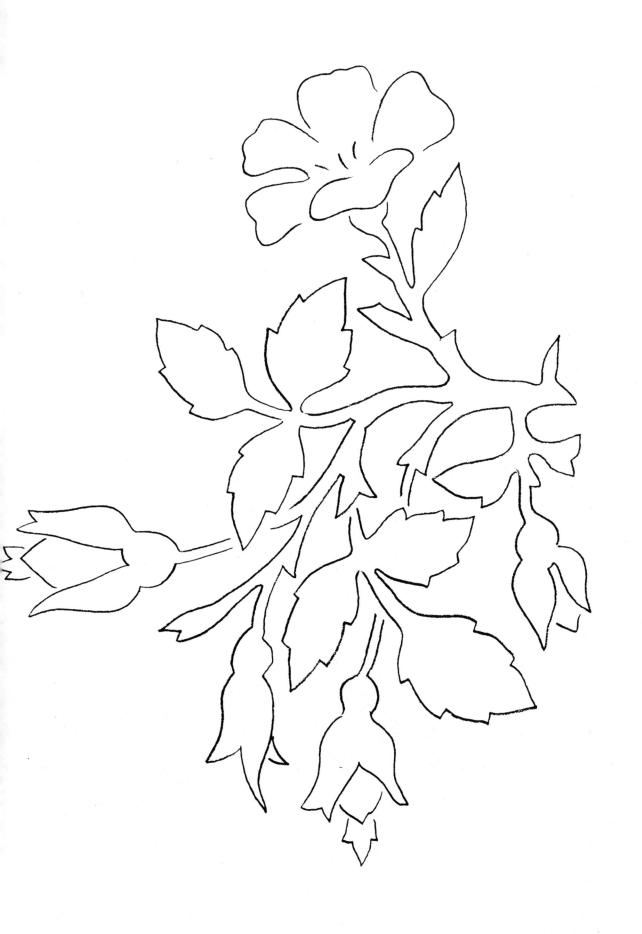

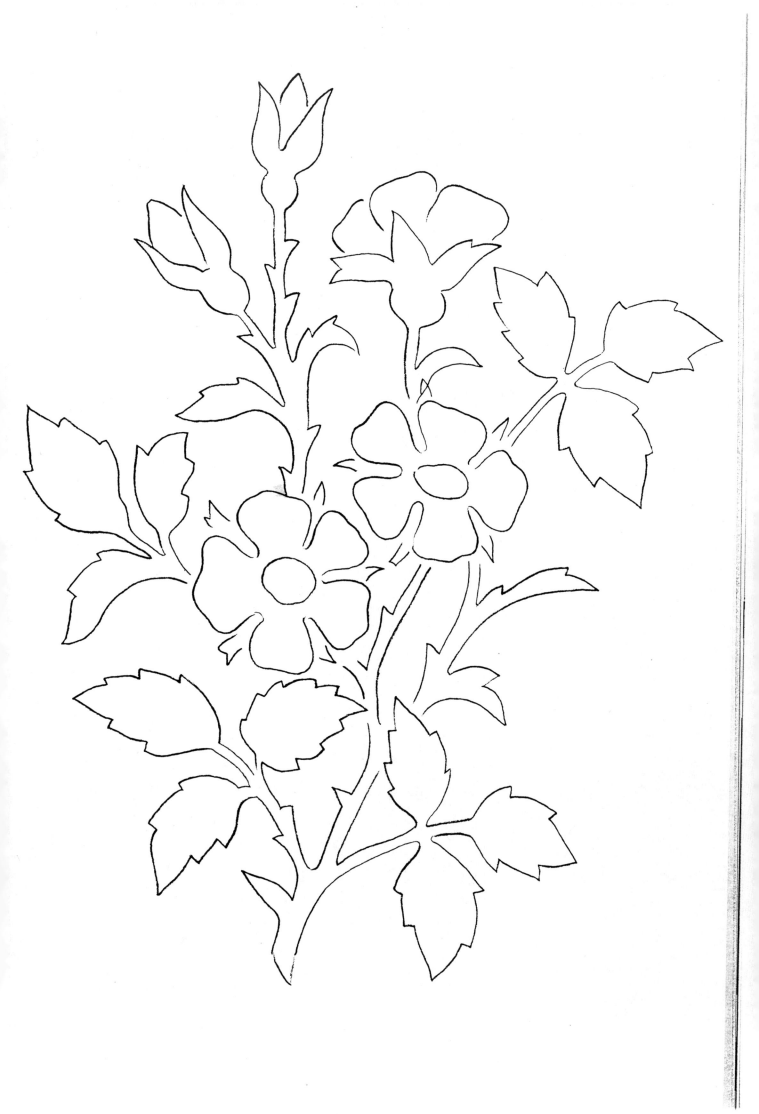

THIS PAPER PROTECTS THE BLUE TRANSFER
PAPER USED TO TRACE DOWN THE MOTIFS
ONTO ANY SURFACE.

CAREFULLY PRISE OPEN THE STAPLE IN THE
MIDDLE OF THIS PIECE OF PAPER USING A
BLUNT KNIFE. YOU WILL THEN BE ABLE TO
REMOVE THE TRANSFER PAPER AND TRACE-
DOWN MOTIFS WITHOUT DAMAGING THE
REST OF THE BOOK.

MOST PEOPLE FIND IT EASIEST TO USE THE
TRANSFER PAPER IF IT IS CUT DOWN TO A
SIZE THAT ROUGHLY MATCHES THE SIZE OF
THE MOTIF BEING TRACED DOWN. HOWEVER,
DO MAKE SURE YOU KEEP A PIECE OF
TRANSFER PAPER LARGE ENOUGH TO USE WITH
THE BIGGEST OF THE MOTIFS IN THIS BOOK.
THE TRANSFER PAPER IS RE-USABLE, AND BY
MOVING IT AROUND AS YOU TRACE THE
DESIGNS, YOU SHOULD FIND THAT THERE IS
AN AMPLE SUPPLY FOR YOUR NEEDS. IF YOU
DO RUN OUT OF TRANSFER PAPER, OR IF YOU
LOSE IT, FURTHER SHEETS CAN BE BOUGHT
FROM ARTISTS' SUPPLIERS.

IT'S ALSO A WISE PRECAUTION TO PHOTOCOPY
THE TRACING PATTERNS, SO THAT YOU DON'T
WORRY ABOUT LOSING OR DAMAGING THE
ORIGINALS. A PHOTOCOPIER WILL ALLOW YOU
TO ENLARGE OR REDUCE THE SIZE OF THE
MOTIFS, TOO, ENABLING YOU TO SCALE THE
DESIGNS ACCORDING TO THE SIZE OF YOUR
PIECES OF FURNITURE.

6 WORKING FROM LEFT TO RIGHT (IF YOU ARE RIGHT HANDED), ADD THE ROSES AND BUDS. USE THE FLAT BRUSH AND POINTED BRUSH AND THE TECHNIQUE OF SHADING PREVIOUSLY SHOWN.

7 NOW THAT ALMOST ALL THE FLOWERS ARE COMPLETE THE RICHNESS OF THE OVERALL EFFECT IS APPARENT. NOTE, AS BEFORE, HOW THE FREE HAND IS USED AS A 'REST'.

8 THE YELLOW CENTRES HAVE BEEN ADDED AND NOW A FINE BRUSH AND DOTS OF COLOUR J ARE USED TO PAINT IN THE STAMENS, THE FINAL DETAILS IN THE COMPOSITION.

A POT-POURRI OF DECORATIVE IDEAS

Posies of roses gain pungency from simple decorative 'framing'.

These detail pictures illustrate how much mileage can be obtained from one set of floral motifs, simply by varying the intensity of colour and tone, changing the background colour, or by re-arranging the posies and sprays themselves to create shapes that fill and dramatize a particular space, such as the washstand back and top, a cupboard door panel or our sweepingly curvaceous bedhead. Time spent jigging your motifs about on the surface for the best effect is never wasted.

A CHARMINGLY SIMPLE BEDSIDE CUPBOARD GAINS A NEW DIMENSION WHEN PAINTED THE PALEST OF GREENS, WITH THE TOP AND BASE IN DARK GREEN AND A DARK GREEN LINE USED TO 'FRAME' THE DECORATED DOOR PANEL.

THE WATERCOLOURS HERE ARE MORE VIVID AND JUICIER, ALLOWING A LIVELIER ACCENTING OF THE WHOLE PIECE WITH BANDS OF MOULDING PICKED OUT IN VIVID PINK. NOTE HOW CLEVERLY THE ROSE CLUSTERS HAVE BEEN SYMMETRICALLY ARRANGED TO ECHO THE CUT-OUT PROFILE OF THE BEDSTEAD ITSELF.

THE FLOWER ARRANGER'S ART

By re-arranging, pruning, or reversing patterns, a few designs can be tailored to fit and glamourize all those blank surfaces crying out for imaginative decoration.

Any really pale colour will make a suitable base coat for our English Rose collection, whether it's the palest pink, blue, yellow, cream, green or ivory. Make sure the base colour is truly opaque (at least two coats) and well smoothed with wet-and-dry paper because such fine work demands a well-prepared ground. Spray varnish each decorative passage on completion for extra protection. Lining and picking out should use the same gouache and gum arabic combination, in harmonizing colours, but don't overdo this. A final 'antiquing' finish, using matt or eggshell polyurethane varnish lightly tinted with oil tube colour (oily varnish needs oily tints), will soften and integrate the whole scheme, and make it look even more natural.

WHAT COULD BE PRETTIER THAN A BED OF MINIATURE INDOOR ROSES CONTAINED IN A PLANTER LIKE THIS? THE PIECE COULD BE FRENCH, AND THE REGULARLY REPEATED MOTIF, 'TWISTED RIBBON' BORDERS AND 'PICKING OUT' OF THE TURNED LEGS ALL CONTRIBUTE TO ITS FRIVOLOUS CHARM.

VAGUELY HEART-SHAPED ARRANGEMENTS OF THE BASIC MOTIF NICELY EMPHASIZE THE CURVES OF THE CUT-OUT PINE BEDHEAD AND FOOT, WHILE A VIVID PINK 'PICKS OUT' DETAILS OF TURNED MOULDING ON THE LEGS AND POSTS.

ROSES, OLD AND NEW, SEEM TO
COMPLEMENT ONE ANOTHER IN
DECORATION AS EFFORTLESSLY AS
THEY DO IN NATURE. HERE, OLD
PAINTED CERAMICS AND TODAY'S
WATERCOLOUR PAINTING ON THE
VICTORIAN WASHSTAND EMBRACE
LIKE OLD FRIENDS.

Can you ever have too much of a good thing? Half the fun of our transfer patterns lies in the ease with which they can be adapted. Use them not just to dress up larger items of furniture but also to glorify little things — such as trays and boxes — for a thought-through effect which makes a room look cherished.

PS: Personalized 'trifles' like these make brilliant gifts - just add an initial or two.

FLOWERY BREAKFAST TRAYS AND AN ENCHANTING HEART-SHAPED BOX ARE PRETTY ENOUGH TO TAKE THE STING OUT OF WAKING UP. IN THEIR SMALL COMPASS THEY ILLUSTRATE HOW THE SAME MOTIFS CAN BE USED TO DIFFERENT EFFECT, LOOSELY OR FORMALLY, IN VIVID COLOURS OR AS FADED AS THE LAST ROSE OF SUMMER.

A MELTINGLY PRETTY EARLY-MORNING VIGNETTE CONSISTS OF NOTHING MORE THAN ONE OF OUR ROSE-WREATHED TRAYS NUDGED UP TO THE PAINTED BEDHEAD.

A CONVINCING DEMONSTRATION ON A
SMALL SCALE OF THE IMPORTANCE OF
'FRAMING' EVEN (OR ESPECIALLY) THE
MOST ETHEREAL STYLE OF PAINTED
DECORATION. LINING ON THE BOX AND
WASHSTAND, IN PINK AND GREEN, HOLDS
THE WHOLE SCHEME TOGETHER. PRACTISE
THIS FIRST ON PAPER WITH A FINE BRUSH.
BEGINNERS' LINES MAY WOBBLE A
FRACTION, BUT AIM FOR A CARELESS
HANDPAINTED EFFECT, WHICH IS
ALWAYS MUCH MORE PREFERABLE TO
FACTORY-FINISHED EXACTNESS.

THE SOFTER, MORE WATERY RENDERING OF
THE ENGLISH ROSE PATTERNS ON THIS
LITTLE OVAL TRAY HARKS BACK TO THE
TREATMENT OF OUR PAINTED SCREEN. THE
DIFFERENCE IS ONE OF TRANSPARENT
DECORATION (MORE GUM ARABIC, LESS
GOUACHE COLOUR) AS MUCH AS OF A
LOOSER ARRANGEMENT.

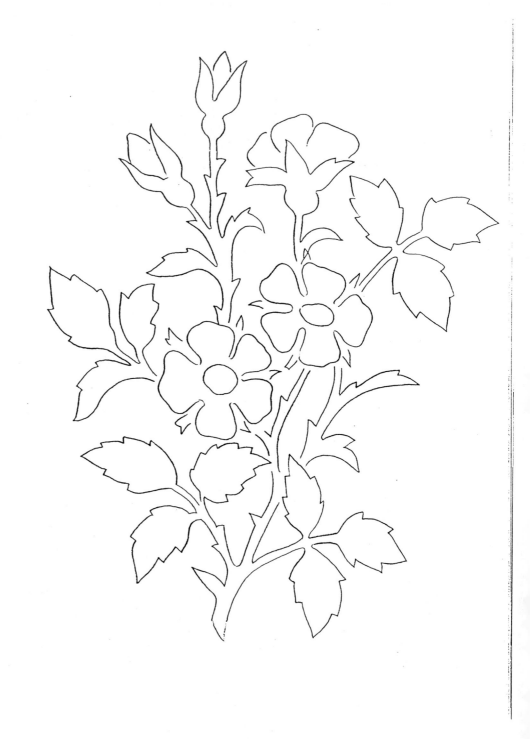

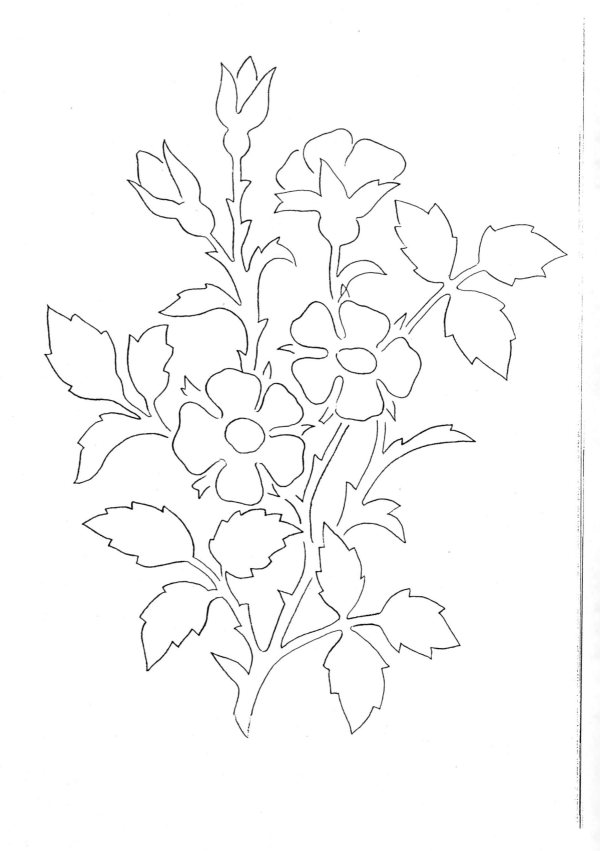

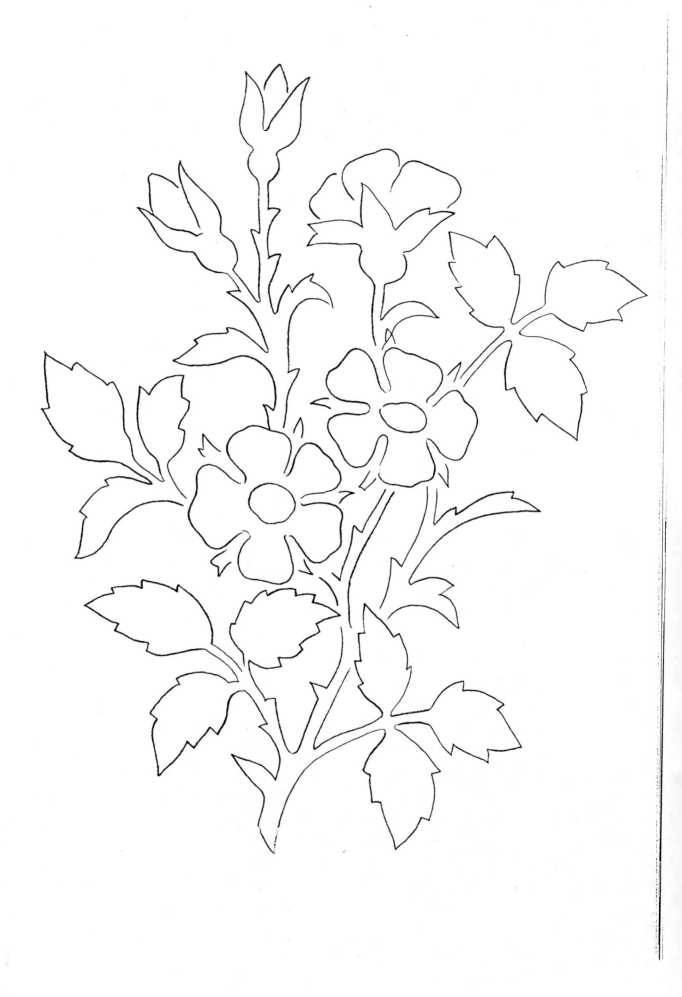

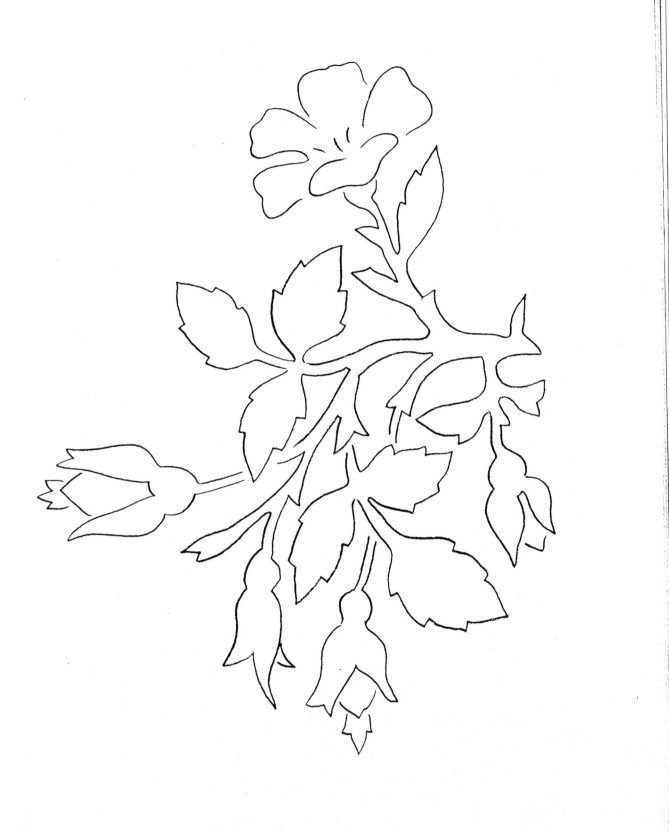

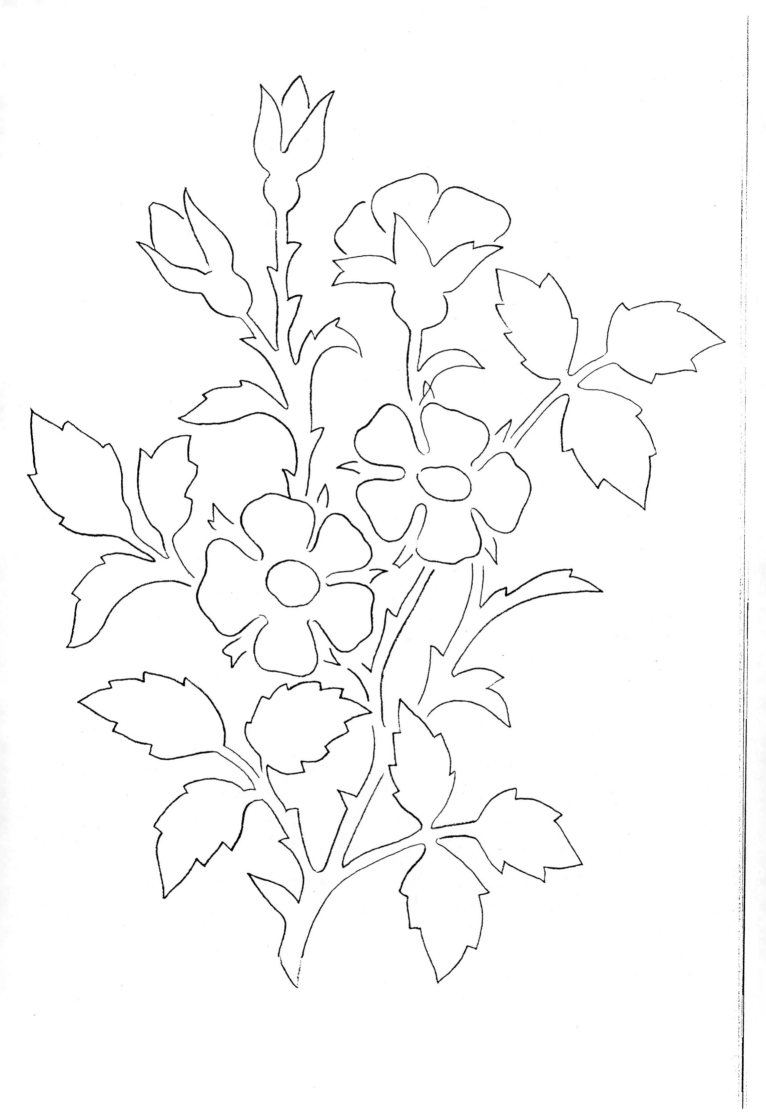